SET TO WORSHIP THE ANTICHRIST 666

God sends them a powerful delusion so that they will believe the lie.
2 Thessalonians 2:11 (NIV)

SET UP TO WORSHIP THE ANTICHRIST 666

God sends them a powerful delusion so that they will believe the lie.
2 Thessalonians 2:11 (NIV)

JACK STONE

Outskirts Press, Inc.
Denver, Colorado

Scripture marked (NIV) taken from the HOLY BIBLE, NEW INTERNATIONAL VERSION. Copyright 1973,1978,1984 International Bible Society. Used by permission of Zondervan Bible Publishers.
Scripture marked (KJV) taken from the King James Version.
Scripture marked (TNIV) taken from the HOLY BIBLE, TODAY'S NEW INTERNATIONAL VERSION®. Copyright © 2001, 2005 by International Bible Society®. Used by permission of International Bible Society®. All rights reserved worldwide.

The opinions expressed in this manuscript are solely the opinions of the author and do not represent the opinions or thoughts of the publisher. The author has represented and warranted full ownership and/or legal right to publish all the materials in this book.

Set Up To Worship The Antichrist
God sends them a powerful delusion so that they will believe the lie. 2 Thessalonians 2:11 (NIV).
All Rights Reserved.
Copyright © 2009 Jack Stone
V9.0

This book may not be reproduced, transmitted, or stored in whole or in part by any means, including graphic, electronic, or mechanical without the express written consent of the publisher except in the case of brief quotations embodied in critical articles and reviews.

Outskirts Press, Inc.
http://www.outskirtspress.com

ISBN: 978-1-4327-2894-6

Outskirts Press and the "OP" logo are trademarks belonging to Outskirts Press, Inc.

PRINTED IN THE UNITED STATES OF AMERICA

Dedicated to the millions of souls, having lost faith in the institutions created by man, are turning to The Creator of the universe, our God, the True God and earnestly seeking to know His plan for bringing this age to a close.

John 8:32 And ye shall know the truth, and the truth shall make you free.

Contents

Foreword		ix
Chapter One	Jesus Christ or Antichrist	1
Chapter Two	God Sends Them A Powerful Delusion	15
Chapter Three	In My Father's House	19
Chapter Four	What Jesus Taught	27
Chapter Five	When We Put on Immortality	35
Chapter Six	Absent From Body, Present With The Lord	43
Chapter Seven	What Billy Graham Believes	47
Chapter Eight	Jesus Gave Us a Sign	51
Chapter Nine	It Is Finished	57
Chapter Ten	No Rebuilt Temple Needed	73
Chapter Eleven	None Saved During Tribulation	77
Chapter Twelve	Conflicting Conclusions	91
Chapter Thirteen	New Testament Church Is Israel	95
Chapter Fourteen	Antichrist Comes	105
Chapter Fifteen	Jesus Christ Comes	109

Foreword

Just as God visited earth almost 2000 years ago and lived in a body that we call Jesus, the Bible tells us Satan is likewise going to visit earth and live in a body that we call the Antichrist. The Bible also tells us that Jesus is coming again to earth. So we have two very important visitations: one by God and the other by Satan. The very important question is: **which one comes first?**

This book will separate fact (Bible) from fiction (man's theories). It will help you discover that God told us who will come first and how to recognize the impostor from the real Christ.

The purpose of this book is to point you to the truth of the end times revealed in the Bible which has been misinterpreted. If we are truly living in the last of the last days as many proclaim, the information contained herein is vitally important because of what is shortly to come upon the earth. If this is not the time of the end, it is still important to pass these truths on to future generations.

There are different interpretations about how the end of this age will unfold. The emphasis in this book will be on God's plan as laid out in the Bible. His plan was widely accepted by the great scholars of the Bible such as Matthew Henry, Charles Spurgeon, Adam Clarke, John Wesley, George Whitfield and many others. These men believed and taught God's plan which will be examined here.

Just as creative minds of the last two hundred years have successfully redefined Jesus for millions, some going so far as to strip Christ of His Deity, others have chosen to alter the end-time teachings of the Bible as taught by the greats of Christianity, like those mentioned above. It will be demonstrated that Henry, Spurgeon, Wesley, Whitfield and many others were not wrong in their beliefs and teachings about this subject.

Questions should be asked such as: "Why are we discarding what these great men of Christianity believed and taught?" "What new evidence do we have that they did not have?"

Many beliefs, widely held today, were not supported in the sermons and writings of these great men of God. Why? Because those same beliefs had not been created during the lifetimes of these men. We need to follow Paul's advice: *Prove all things; hold fast that which is good. (1 Thessalonians 5:21)*.

C.I. Scofield (1843-1921) is largely responsible for changing the established end-time beliefs held by the aforementioned theologians and many other giants of Biblical knowledge, all of whom, came before Scofield. He said in the Introduction to his first edition of THE SCOFIELD REFERENCE BIBLE published in 1909, "... that all of the many excellent and useful editions of the Word of God **left much to be desired**".

Scofield decided that the King James Bible was inadequate to reveal God's message in the English language. It needed his help. On the title page, below the words "Authorized Version" of THE SCOFIELD REFERENCE BIBLE, he placed the following words: "WITH A NEW SYSTEM OF CONNECTED TOPICAL REFERENCES TO ALL THE GREATER THEMES OF SCRIPTURES WITH ANNOTATIONS, REVISED MARGINAL RENDERINGS, SUMMARIES, DEFINITIONS, CHRONOLOGY, AND INDEX TO WHICH ARE ADDED HELPS AT HARD PLACES, EXPLANATIONS OF SEEMING DISCREPANCIES, AND A NEW SYSTEM OF PARAGRAPHS".

With his new Reference Bible, Scofield changed what people had believed. These SUMMARIES of Scofield have been read and elevated to the status of being "divine", pioneering the way for the widely held view that the Antichrist will make a seven year peace treaty with the Jews and then break it after 3.5 years. It will be demonstrated, herein, that that view and others, widely held today, propagated by Scofield can not be substantiated by the text of the Bible, only by the notes of Scofield. C.I. Scofield turned that teaching and others into "gospel", not Christ, not Paul, not Peter nor John.

William Tyndale (1494-1536) was burned at the stake for

translating the Bible into the English of his day so that common people could read the Word of God. Much of Tyndale's work is found in the King James Version used today. What would Tyndale think of Scofield's statement that Tyndale's translation "left much to be desired". Tyndale gave his life for that translation. More importantly, what would Tyndale think of Scofield's summaries? He probably wouldn't agree with much of it.

A story goes that a government employee, whose job was to detect counterfeit bills, was asked if he spent a lot of time studying the bogus bills. His reply was no. He spent his time studying the real ones. Then it was easy to spot the counterfeit ones.

Likewise, we will study God's Word, and then it will be easy to detect that which is contrary to His Word.

An eternal debt of gratitude goes to London-based missionaries, Dirk Wood and Steve Same, who introduced Bible reading to my wife Sandra and me. Their method is very simple: start at page one and read every page until the last page and then start again at page one. In preparing for this task, I have read every Word in the Bible from Genesis to Revelation at least ten times using their example. I have followed the words of Jesus in Matthew 7:7-8. I have asked and it has been given to me. I have sought and I have found. I have knocked, and I believe, doors in the Word have been opened.

This book is the product of ten years of diligently searching the scriptures for answers to questions about the end of the age and Christ's return. You will see many passages quoted from the Bible. This is done for two reasons. First, no one can improve upon what God has written. Second, if you disagree, you are not at odds with me, but with God.

God is the author of this book. My pleasure has been to serve as editor. It is a must-read because many of you will not read the Bible, but you will read much of the "Bible" in this book. Don't remain a vegetarian, devour the meat that can only be found in His Word.

We will gather evidence from the Bible about the "end of the age" and how we need to prepare for those events to come upon the earth before the "coming of the Lord". Today, more than ever before, we need to know, with certainty, what God told us long ago about how the end of this age will unfold. We are living in the days Paul described here:

*For the time will come when men will not put up with sound doctrine. Instead, to suit their own desires, they will gather around them a great number of teachers to say what their **itching ears** want to hear. They will turn their ears away from the truth and turn aside to myths. 2 Timothy 4:3-4 (NIV)*

Many of you will be offended just as the scripture says: **Have I now become your enemy by telling you the truth?** *(Galatians 4:16(TNIV))*.

Also, the Apostle Paul said: ..., **Satan himself is transformed into an angel of light. Therefore it is no great thing if his ministers also be transformed as the ministers of righteousness ....** *2 Corinthians 11:14-15.*

Take no man's word for anything, mine included. Prove everything from the Bible. Yes, there are wicked men passing themselves off as ministers of the Gospel of Jesus Christ. The purpose of this book is to get you to study the book that really matters, the Bible. *"All Scripture is God-breathed and is useful for teaching, rebuking, correcting and training in righteousness" (2 Timothy 3:16 (NIV).*

God has only one scenario for the end of the age and His return. He described it in great detail in His Book. Truth in His Word must be sought with a hundred times more diligence than the pursuit of money. Truth worth seeking comes from the Creator of this universe.

My desire is that when our Lord and Savior Jesus Christ comes after the trying days of the tribulation, I can say to Him, "I did my best to warn them not to worship the impostor".

Who Comes First: Jesus Christ or Antichrist

1

William Bell Riley (1861-1942) was known as "The Grand Old Man of Fundamentalism". Dr. Riley began his ministry as pastor of the First Baptist Church, Minneapolis and served there for forty-five years, and another five as pastor emeritus. Dr. Riley wrote a number of texts on Christian Evangelism and founded the Northwestern Bible Training School along with an Evangelical Seminary.

Dr. Riley said, "It is my candid conviction that no more serious obligation rests upon any living preacher of the present century than that of so clearly and carefully interpreting prophecy as to enable his people to distinguish the Antichrist from the Christ" (206).

How many sermons have you heard explaining how to distinguish the Antichrist from the Christ? The Apostle Paul, in his sermon to the church at Antioch, said:

Acts 13:27 (NIV) The people of Jerusalem and their rulers did not recognize Jesus, yet in condemning him they fulfilled the words of the prophets that are read every Sabbath.

This is an example of the importance of understanding. The Jews did not recognize Jesus as the promised Messiah, although they read about Him every Sabbath. The Jewish priests had the Words of the prophet Micah, who predicted that the long-awaited Messiah would be born in Bethlehem (Micah 5:2). They had the Words of the prophet Isaiah who predicted the Messiah would be born of a virgin (Isaiah 7:14). Isaiah, provided in chapter 53, the most detailed description of the promised Messiah.

Isaiah 53

*3 He is **despised and rejected of men**; a man of sorrows, and acquainted with grief: and we hid as it were our faces from him; he was despised, and we esteemed him not. 4 Surely **he hath borne our griefs, and carried our sorrows**: 5 But **he was wounded for our transgressions, he was bruised for our iniquities**: the chastisement of our peace was upon him; and **with his stripes we are healed**. 6 All we like sheep have gone astray; we have turned every one to his own way; and **the LORD hath laid on him the iniquity of us all.***

*10 Yet it pleased **the LORD to bruise him**; ... because **he hath poured out his soul unto death: and he was numbered with the transgressors; and he bare the sin of many, and made intercession for the transgressors.***

The Words of Isaiah above do not describe a King coming in great power and glory to setup a worldly kingdom. No, they describe a suffering servant, who came to earth, to take upon Himself the sins of the world. His kingdom was not of this world. The guilt for not understanding and believing that Jesus was the long-awaited Messiah is put at the feet of the educated: the priests, the teachers of the law, the Pharisees and the scribes. <u>Why did this educated group, who had the honor of seeing our God in bodily form, miss the truth written by Isaiah</u>? The lay people of that day did not have the Words of the prophets, for the most part, or the ability to read them. They only had the words coming from the mouths of the educated group.

The guilt for unbelief and false beliefs, today, rests totally with those who have the Holy Words of God. We must take responsibility ourselves .

As mentioned earlier, William Tyndale died so that we could have the Word of God in our English language. He is one of many who have paid an enormous price in order that we could personally have access to the Word of God. Included in this group are the many, who have sacrificed much, in order to deliver the Words of God in so many different languages other than English.

Just as it happened with the coming of Jesus, you will see that the Word of God tells us the same thing is going to happen again, but this time, the one many people, even some Christians, won't recognize is the Antichrist, the impostor of Christ.

The Bible tells us in great detail:

- The Antichrist will make his appearance before Jesus Christ returns for His Followers.
- How to recognize the impostor, so you will not be deceived.

The Apostle Paul tells the church at Thessalonica, in his second letter to them, that the Antichrist will make his appearance **before** our Lord and Savior Jesus Christ comes and gathers together His believers.

2 Thessalonians 2:1 (NIV) Concerning the coming of our Lord Jesus Christ and our being gathered to him, we ask you, brothers, 2 not to become easily unsettled or alarmed by some prophecy, report or letter supposed to have come from us, saying that the day of the Lord has already come. 3 Don't let anyone deceive you in any way, for that day will not come until the rebellion occurs and the man of lawlessness is revealed, the man doomed to destruction.

Paul told his brethren that *"the coming of our Lord Jesus Christ and our being gathered to him"* will occur on the *"day of the Lord"*. The term, *"day of the Lord"* was well understood in Paul's day. Paul had taught them about it using the words of the Old Testament prophets: Isaiah, Ezekiel, Joel, Amos, Obadiah, Zephaniah, Zechariah and Malachi. The phrase "day of the Lord" occurs 18 times in the Old Testament and 5 times in the New Testament. It occurs a sixth time when you include "day of Christ" in 2 Thessalonians 2:2, which you should. We must all agree that Jesus Christ is Lord.

Joel 1:15 (KJV) Alas for the day! for the <u>day of the LORD</u> is at hand, and as a <u>destruction from the Almighty</u> shall it come. Joel 2:30-32 The sun shall be turned into darkness, and the moon into blood, before the great and terrible <u>day of the LORD</u> come. And it shall come to pass, that <u>whosoever shall call on the name of the LORD shall be delivered:</u> for in mount Zion and in Jerusalem shall be deliverance, as the LORD hath said, and in the <u>remnant whom the LORD shall call</u>.

The prophet Joel's prophecy above is repeated by Peter in his message on the day of Pentecost. Peter substantiated that salvation to all followers of Christ would come on the "day of the Lord".

*Acts 2:20 The sun shall be turned into darkness, and the moon into blood, before the great and notable **day of the Lord** come: 21 And it shall come to pass, that whosoever shall call on the name of the Lord shall be saved.*

The Life Application Bible, describes *"day of the Lord"* as follows: "The 'day of the Lord' is a future time when God will intervene directly and dramatically in world affairs. Predicted and discussed often in the Old Testament ..., the day of the Lord will include both punishment and blessing." (2175).

Paul told the church at Thessalonica not to be deceived, that the *"day of the Lord"*, **when Christ returns for them, will not come until after the man of lawlessness, the Antichrist, is revealed and the great rebellion against God takes place.** (2 Thess. 2:1-3). Paul was trying to correct a false letter or teaching that the "day of the Lord" had already come and they were not taken. The Christians had been previously taught that Christ would return for them on the *"day of the Lord"*. Paul made it very clear that the Antichrist would make his appearance before Christ returns for His followers on the *"day of the Lord"*.

In the introduction to 2 Thessalonians of the Open Bible we find, "The second chapter is written to correct the fallacious teaching that the day of the Lord has already come upon the Thessalonian church. This teaching, coupled with the afflictions they have been suffering, is causing a great disturbance among the believers who wonder when they 'will be gathered together to meet him' (2:1; 1 Thes. 4:13-18)." (1600-1).

Continuing on with Paul's letter, he tells the church at Thessalonica:

2 Thessalonians 2:4-5 (NIV) He [Antichrist] will oppose and will exalt himself over everything that is called God or is worshiped, so that he sets himself up in God's temple, proclaiming himself to be God. Don't you remember that when I was with you I used to tell you these things?

In Nelson's New Illustrated Bible Dictionary 1995 in its description of the book of 2 Thessalonians, we find, "Paul appeals to them to be levelheaded during the time of trouble and warns Christians not to despair when they see the Antichrist pretending to be God (2 Thess. 2:4)" (1245).

Paul told his brothers in Christ to expect to see the Antichrist masquerading as God.

Paul had discussed *"day of the Lord"* with the believers, so they were familiar with it. He did not need to define it for them. How many preachers today teach their congregations about the "day of the Lord"? Paul had taught the believers what the Old Testament prophets had said about it. God thought it was important enough to have eight of His prophets listed above write about it. Paul has clearly told the believers that the Antichrist will come before "*the coming of our Lord Jesus Christ and our being gathered to him*". He described **that day** as the "*day of the Lord*" *(2 Thessalonians 2:1-2)*. Continuing on with Paul's letter, he tells the church at Thessalonica, about the "great lie", which is, that people will believe the Antichrist is Jesus Christ.

2 Thessalonians 2:9 (NIV) The coming of the lawless one will be in accordance with the work of Satan displayed in all kinds of counterfeit miracles, signs and wonders, 10 and in every sort of evil that deceives those who are perishing. They perish because they refuse to love the truth and so be saved. 11 For this reason God sends them a powerful delusion so that they will believe the lie 12 and so that all will be condemned who have not believed the truth but have delighted in wickedness.

Young's Literal Translation: 2 Thessalonians 2:11 *and because of this shall God send to them a working of delusion, for their believing the lie, that they may be judged- all who did not believe the truth, but were well pleased in the unrighteousness.*

"The 'lie' is not just any lie but the great lie that the man of lawlessness is God ...", according to the Holman Bible Handbook (734). Paul is saying that many will believe the Antichrist, the man of lawlessness, is Jesus.

How could anyone believe the man of lawlessness (Antichrist) is God (Jesus)?

Maybe it's because some Christians have been told they will be secretly snatched up and taken to heaven before the tribulation starts and the Antichrist makes his appearance. Then, after seven years in heaven with Christ, they will come back to earth with Christ at the end of the tribulation.

These believers are not taught that before Christ returns for them, they should expect to see the Antichrist come and perform *all kinds of counterfeit miracles, signs and wonders* (*2 Thess. 2:9*) and proclaim he is God (*2 Thess. 2:4*). Because they have NOT been told ahead of time, many will believe the Antichrist **is Jesus Christ, particularly when they see the Antichrist performing miracles.** These miracles will be very real and profound, such as a quadriplegic receiving all new limbs instantly. Some Christians will worship the Antichrist as God, because they have been taught to expect Jesus to come first. Yes, they are looking for Jesus, not the impostor, the Antichrist. They will be ready to embrace the Antichrist. **They have been setup to believe the great lie of 2 Thessalonians 2:11**. They will worship the Antichrist as Jesus Christ and be eternally damned.

The question has been raised: "How can Christians who expect the rapture to occur before the tribulation worship the Antichrist?" The answer is:

2 Thessalonians 2:4-5 (NIV) He [Antichrist] will oppose and will exalt himself over everything that is called God or is worshiped, so that he sets himself up in God's temple, proclaiming himself to be God.

The deception will be that God's temple is NOT a rebuilt temple in Jerusalem. No, Paul told us what the temple of God is.

1 Corinthians 3:16 *Know ye not that ye are the temple of God, and that the Spirit of God dwelleth in you?*

2 Corinthians 6:16 *And what agreement hath the temple of God with idols? for ye are the temple of the living God ...*

The Apostle Paul has just told us the Antichrist will set himself up in a Christian Church and will claim to be God. He will be performing miracles so profound it will fool many people. Even Christians will be fooled, because of the miracles they will see the Antichrist perform. They will believe the Antichrist is Jesus.

The problems soon to come upon the world will be of such magnitude that people everywhere, Christians and non-Christians will be looking for answers. When President Obama was in Germany in 2008 during his campaign for president, he was almost given a messiah's welcome. Some even call him messiah. As the global economic chaos, we now face, worsens with more and more people finding themselves jobless, homeless and hungry, the quest for solutions will reach a new level.

People will be looking for "the man" to lead them out of their misery, to give them relief. They will be ripe for the deception of the Antichrist. They have been setup to believe this great lie, that the

Antichrist is God (Jesus), that Paul warned us about. The Apostle John wrote, in the book of Revelation, what Christ dictated. Here, Jesus warns us about the Antichrist. In this passage, the dragon is Satan and the beast is the Antichrist.

Revelation 13:1 And I stood upon the sand of the sea, and saw a <u>beast</u> rise up out of the sea, ... 2 ... and the <u>dragon</u> gave him [beast] his power, and his seat, and great authority. 3 ... and all the world wondered after the <u>beast</u>. 4 ... and they worshipped the <u>beast</u>, saying, Who is like unto the <u>beast</u>? who is able to make war with him? 5 And there was given unto him a mouth speaking great things and blasphemies; and power was given unto him to continue forty and two months. 6 And he opened his mouth in blasphemy against God, to blaspheme his name, and his tabernacle, and them that dwell in heaven. 7 And it was given unto him to make war with the saints, and to overcome them: and power was given him over all kindreds, and tongues, and nations. 8 And all that dwell upon the earth shall worship him, whose names are not written in the book of life of the Lamb slain from the foundation of the world. 9 If any man have an ear, let him hear.

The book of Revelation is included in our Bible as a warning from Jesus of the way He intends to bring this age to an end. Note verse 9 above, you do have an ear so listen to Jesus.

Returning to the Apostle Paul's letter to the church at Thessalonica, he issues a stern warning to not let anyone deceive you.

2 Thessalonians 2:1 (NIV) Concerning the coming of our Lord Jesus Christ and our being gathered to him, we ask you, brothers, 2 not to become easily unsettled or alarmed by some prophecy, report or letter supposed to have come from us, saying that the day of the Lord has already come. 3 <u>Don't let anyone deceive you in any way, for that day will not come until the rebellion occurs and the man of lawlessness is revealed</u>, the man doomed to destruction.

Paul clearly warns us to not be deceived, that the Antichrist, the man of lawlessness, will come before the ***day of the Lord,*** when Jesus returns for His Followers. However, many are claiming, "The next event on God's prophetic calendar is the rapture of the church".

Once again, Paul tells his brothers in the church in 2 Thessalonians 2:1-3, that **before Jesus comes and gathers up His followers, the Antichrist will be revealed.** You have clearly seen that the Apostle

Paul was telling the church at Thessalonica that the impostor, the Antichrist, will make his appearance before our savior, Christ Jesus comes for them.

Revelation 14:9-11 warns us that those who worship the Antichrist, the man of lawlessness, or receive the "mark of the beast" will be tormented with fire and brimstone eternally. Satan is described as the dragon, the old serpent, and the Devil in Revelation 12:9. The dragon gives power to the beast in Revelation 13:1-2. This same beast is also referred to as the man of sin or the Antichrist. So the "mark of the beast" is the mark of Satan. This mark means you will spend eternity with Satan in the "lake of fire".

Marvin Rosenthal, in his book, <u>The Pre-Wrath Rapture of The Church</u>, while speaking of the church on earth during the period of time commonly referred to as Daniel's seventieth week in which the Antichrist will reign, writes: "The church will enter that period unprepared, spiritually naked, vulnerable, and ripe for the Antichrist's deception. The psychological implications will be disastrous. A questioning of the trustworthiness of the Word of God will naturally follow. It will be a spiritual catastrophe– a *Pearl Harbor* of incalculable proportions– a satanically planned sneak attack" (281-2).

Once again, why will the church Not be prepared? Because they have been taught they will be snatched up and taken to heaven before any of this begins. The real danger of this teaching is given to us by these Words of Christ: *"When trouble or **persecution** comes because of the word, he quickly falls away"* (Matthew 13:21).

Let's study the verses from the Bible used most often to support the theory of an escape before the tribulation begins. You can confirm from their writings, proponents of that theory say that First Thessalonians 4:13-18 gives the most comprehensive account of the rapture of the church in the Bible. Let's examine this passage of scripture:

1 Thessalonians 4:13 (NIV) Brothers, we do not want you to be ignorant about those who fall asleep, or to grieve like the rest of men, who have no hope. 14 We believe that Jesus died and rose again and so we believe that God will bring with Jesus those who have fallen asleep in him. 15 According to the Lord's own word, we tell you that we who are still alive, who are left till the coming of the Lord, will certainly not precede those who have fallen asleep. 16 For the Lord himself will come down from heaven, with a loud command, with the voice of the archangel and with the trumpet call of

God, and the dead in Christ will rise first. 17 After that, we who are still alive and are left will be caught up together with them in the clouds to meet the Lord in the air. And so we will be with the Lord forever. 18 Therefore encourage each other with these words.

When the Bible was written it was not divided into chapters and verses as we have it today. Stephen Langston, Archbishop of Canterbury, divided the Bible into chapters in 1220. Robert Stephanus of Paris divided the Bible into verses in 1551.

Paul's letter continues into chapter 5, so let's keep reading until we finish the topic Paul is discussing. Then, we shall understand what he was telling those church members.

*1 Thessalonians 5:1 (NIV) Now, brothers, about times and dates we do not need to write to you, 2 for you know very well that **the day of the Lord** will come like a thief in the night. 3 While people are saying, "Peace and safety," destruction will come on them suddenly, as labor pains on a pregnant woman, and they will not escape. 4 But you, brothers, are not in darkness so that **this day should surprise you like a thief.***

Paul is continuing on with his letter which left off with 1 Thessalonians 4:18. Keep in mind, Paul was writing this letter to his friends at Thessalonica, just like a letter you might write to some of your friends. Sometimes a sentence or sentences that you write explain or clarify those sentences previous to it. That is the situation here. In the next sentence (5:1), Paul is telling his brothers in Christ that he does not need to tell them when Christ will come back for them, as described in 1 Thess. 4:13-18, because they knew that no one knows when that day will be. Paul described Christ's coming as *"the day of the Lord"* just as he did in 2 Thessalonians 2:2 and that His (Christ's) coming would be secret just as a "thief in the night". He told them <u>it will catch sinners by surprise, but they (Christians) should not be surprised when Jesus comes back and destroys those sinners.</u>

Paul used the Old Testament term, *"the day of the Lord"* to refer to that time when Christ returns to reward his believers and destroy the sinners. Both events happen at the same time. Because Paul did not know when Christ would come back, he wrote to them as though it could happen very soon and they could be alive to witness the "day of the Lord". If they did live to see that day, it would not surprise them, because he had warned them to keep watch. If there was to be a rapture or a "taking away" of believers prior to *"**the day of the**

Lord", there would be no need to warn the brothers about the "day of the Lord" bringing destruction. The brothers would have already left the earth.

According to Nelson's New Illustrated Bible Dictionary 1995, "**The Day of the Lord** will reverse the curse upon the world by bringing judgment to all of God's enemies. The world will be judged by fire (Is.66:16), and all nations will be included in this judgment (Amos 1:3-2:3; Ezek. 25:1-17)" (414).

In the introduction to 1 Thessalonians chapter 4 of the original 1611 King James Bible, we find in old English, "... And vnto this last exhortation is annexed a briefe description of the resurrection, and second comming of Christ to judgement". It was believed in 1611, this scripture referred to the time when Christ will come to judge the ungodly and resurrect his believers. This is in stark contrast to the use made today, which is to substantiate a secret catching away of believers seven years prior to the time Christ comes in judgment.

Read 1 Thessalonians 4:16-17 again. It describes the beginning of the great event in world history called *"the day of the Lord"* which the whole world will see for themselves. Paul says this day will come as a "thief in the night". A thief is not expected, therefore when the thief comes it is a total surprise. In 1 Thessalonians 5:4, Paul says that Christians are not in darkness because they are expecting Christ to return. That day should not surprise Christians, because they have been warned.

That day, "**the day of the Lord**" will be the biggest spectacle the world has ever seen when the glory and majesty of the Lord is displayed before the eyes of everyone on earth. It will be the day when we finally see our Lord, whom we have waited for, face to face. It will be the "blessed hope" that Paul wrote about in his letter to Titus. But it will be the worst day in the lives of all those who have rejected Christ. They will be destroyed.

Back to Titus, Paul explains that the "blessed hope" in Titus 2:13, is *"the hope of eternal life"* (Titus 3:7). In many King James Bibles, you will find a reference in Isaiah 25:9 pointing to Titus 2:13. Isaiah chapters 24-26 speak of salvation after God has brought His judgments upon earth. You can verify this by reading these three chapters in Isaiah.

1 Thessalonians 4:13-18 does NOT support the rapture of the church before the tribulation. The whole text, 1 Thessalonians 4:13- 5:4, shows that Paul told his brothers in the church that the "day of the Lord", would not be a surprise to them when Christ returns to punish sinners and reward His followers. Paul did not speak of an escape for them before the "day of the Lord".

The snatching up of 1 Thessalonians 4:13-5:4 will occur on the "day of the Lord", when Christ comes back after the reign of the Antichrist. Do not let yourself be deceived.

In the Introduction to 2 Thessalonians of the Open Bible we find: "The second chapter is written to correct the fallacious teaching that the day of the Lord has already come upon the Thessalonian church". This teaching, ... is causing a great disturbance among the believers who wonder when they 'will be gathered together to meet him'(2:1; 1 Thes. 4:13-18)" (1600).

Paul had previously taught the Church at Thessalonica that the rapture would take place on the "day of the Lord".

In Paul's second letter, he tells the church at Thessolonica, **that Jesus would comfort them, the believers (vs. 6-7), at the same time he comes back to punish the sinners** (vs. 8-9) as described here:

2 Thessalonians 1:6 (NIV) *God is just: He will pay back trouble to those who trouble you 7 and give relief to you who are troubled, and to us as well. This will happen when the Lord Jesus is revealed from heaven in blazing fire with his powerful angels. 8 He will punish those who do not know God and do not obey the gospel of our Lord Jesus. 9 They will be punished with everlasting destruction and shut out from the presence of the Lord and from the majesty of his power 10 on the day he comes to be glorified in his holy people and to be marveled at among all those who have believed. This includes you, because you believed our testimony to you.*

Paul was Not saying that the Church would be removed from the earth before the Antichrist is revealed.

Let's read again: 2 Thessalonians 2:1 (NIV) *Concerning the coming of our Lord Jesus Christ and our being gathered to him, we ask you, brothers, 2 not to become easily unsettled or alarmed by some prophecy, report or letter supposed to have come from us, saying that the day of the Lord has already come. 3* <u>*Don't let anyone deceive you in any*</u>

way, for that day will not come until the rebellion occurs and the man of lawlessness is revealed, the man doomed to destruction.

Now, you know and can prove with Bible references, to expect the Antichrist BEFORE the day Christ comes back for His believers. That day, when Christ returns is described by Paul, as the "**day of the Lord**". It will be a day when Christ rewards and comforts His own and destroys those who have rejected Him. You will NOT be deceived and will NOT believe the "great lie", that the Antichrist is the real Jesus Christ.

In this world there are many deceivers. A good example is the present state of the world's financial affairs. It's in complete shambles brought on by many deceivers. When it comes to eternal things you must study the Word to see who is right. Opinions must be left to earthly matters. God doesn't have opinions, He has Truth. Just as Jesus is the only way to the Father, there is only one way that the end of the age will unfold. If you are sitting on the fence, it is time to work to find the truth. Truth must be sought with a hundred or a thousand times more effort than all other pursuits. The words *"love of truth"* have a special meaning here.

Proverbs 12:22 (NIV) *The LORD detests lying lips, but he delights in men who are truthful.*

Proverbs 23:23(NIV) *23 Buy the truth and do not sell it; ...*

Jeremiah 5:1(NIV) *"Go up and down the streets of Jerusalem, look around and consider, search through her squares. If you can find but one person who deals honestly and seeks the truth, I will forgive this city.*

Another warning about those that do not seek the truth is found in:

Revelation 22:13 (NIV) *I am Alpha and Omega, the beginning and the end, the first and the last. 14 Blessed are they that do his commandments, that they may have right to the tree of life, and may enter in through the gates into the city. 15 For without are dogs, and sorcerers, and whoremongers, and murderers, and idolaters, and **whosoever loveth and maketh a lie**. 16 I Jesus have sent mine angel to testify unto you these things in the churches.*

If you are NOT a truth seeker, then God may allow you to fall victim to the great impostor, the Antichrist.

The Apostle Paul told the church of Thessalonica in both his letters, 1 and 2 Thessalonians:

1. The Antichrist, will be revealed before the coming of our LORD JESUS CHRIST.

2. The Antichrist will set himself up as God and perform counterfeit miracles.

3. Many, who do not have the <u>love of the truth</u>, will believe the Antichrist is Jesus Christ and worship him and be eternally damned.

4. Paul described "the coming of our Lord Jesus Christ and our being gathered to Him" as the "day of the Lord". This day will not be secret once it starts to happen, but it will come as a "thief in the night".

God Sends Them A Powerful Delusion

2

The delusion sent by God mentioned in the previous chapter needs a closer look. The text is:

2 Thessalonians 2:9 (NIV) The coming of the lawless one will be in accordance with the work of Satan displayed in all kinds of counterfeit miracles, signs and wonders, 10 and in every sort of evil that deceives those who are perishing. They perish because they refuse to love the truth and so be saved. 11 For this reason <u>God sends them a powerful delusion</u> so that they will believe the lie 12 and so that all will be condemned who have not believed the truth but have delighted in wickedness.

The words: ***God sends them a powerful delusion*** is contrary to what many have heard with phrases such as "God is not the author of anything bad". However, this is not what the Bible teaches. The God of the Old Testament is the same in the New Testament.

"I the LORD do not change ..." Malachi 3:6 (NIV).

Jesus Christ is the same yesterday and today and forever. Hebrews 13:8 (NIV).

Jesus said *"I and my Father are one."* John 10:30.

Many are told that God is a loving God and would not allow or cause any bad things to happen to us. However, this teaching is not Biblical. Consider the following scripture:

The LORD did not hesitate to bring the disaster on us, for the LORD our God is righteous in everything he does; yet we have not obeyed him. Daniel 9:14 (TNIV).

When disaster comes to a city, has not the LORD caused it? Amos 3:6 (NIV).

Is it not from the mouth of the Most High that both <u>calamities</u> and good things come? Lamentations 3:38 (NIV)

Those who live in Maroth writhe in pain, waiting for relief, because <u>disaster has come from the LORD, even to the gate of Jerusalem</u>. Micah 1:12 (NIV).

When the commander of the guard found Jeremiah, he said to him, "The LORD your God decreed this disaster for this place. And now the LORD has brought it about; he has done just as he said he would. All this happened because you people sinned against the LORD and did not obey him. ..." Jeremiah 40:2-3 (NIV).

God does allow bad things to happen to people. He has done it in the past. He will do it again.

Another example is recorded in 1 Kings chapter 22. It is a situation where God wants to intervene in the life of King Ahab of Israel. God inquires of His heavenly host to find a way to cause the death of King Ahab. The prophet of God, Micaiah, tells what he saw in the heavenly realm before the throne of God.

*1 Kings 22:19 Micaiah continued, "Therefore hear the word of the LORD : I saw the LORD sitting on his throne with all the host of heaven standing around him on his right and on his left. 20 And the LORD said, 'Who will entice Ahab into attacking Ramoth Gilead and going to his death there?' "One suggested this, and another that. 21 Finally, a spirit came forward, stood before the LORD and said, 'I will entice him.' 22 " 'By what means?' the LORD asked. " '**I will go out and be a lying spirit in the mouths of all his prophets**,' he said. " 'You will succeed in enticing him,' said the LORD. 'Go and do it.' 23 "So now the LORD has put a lying spirit in the mouths of all these prophets of yours. The LORD has decreed disaster for you."*

God sent a spirit to place a lie in the mouths of 400 of the prophets of Ahab, the king of Israel. God had decided it was time for Ahab to die.

God warns us in 2 Thessalonians that He will cause those who refuse to love the truth to be deceived by the Antichrist. This error will cause eternal separation from God.

GOD SENDS THEM A POWERFUL DELUSION ▪ 17

Those with no passion for seeking the truth are included along with those who are in total defiance of God. God wants us all to be truth seekers. You can no longer sit on the fence. You must actively pursue the truth as revealed in His Word. Also we must act upon it as James warned us: *Do not merely listen to the word, and so deceive yourselves. Do what it says.* James 1:22 (NIV)

Usually, when Sodom and Gomorrah are mentioned, it is said that their sin was homosexuality but it needs to be made clear that God was also angry about her other sins: **Now this was the sin of your sister Sodom: She and her daughters were arrogant, overfed and unconcerned; they did not help the poor and needy. 50 They were haughty and did detestable things before me. Therefore I did away with them as you have seen.** Ezekiel 16:49-50 (NIV).

God destroyed Sodom and Gomorrah because of these sins. Is America going to go unpunished? How many times have you heard that greed, that is: love of money, houses, cars, sports, etc. is a sin. It is idolatry.

... *No immoral, impure or **greedy** person—such a man is an idolater—has any inheritance in the kingdom of Christ and of God.* Ephesians 5:3-5 (NIV).

America is guilty. We are about to see that God does allow bad things to happen.

Returning to the lie in 2 Thessalonians 2:11, **"The 'lie' is not just any lie but the great lie that the man of lawlessness is God ..."**, according to the Holman Bible Handbook 1992 (734).

God is going to allow some to fall for the deception of the Antichrist and be eternally condemned. Why? Because they do not have the love of the truth.

3 | In My Father's House

The most comprehensive account of the second coming of Christ in the Bible is given in Matthew chapter 24 and 25. It is also repeated in Mark 13 and Luke 21. It's that important.

However, because these four chapters clearly speak of Christ coming after the tribulation, verses were needed to support a secret escape from the earth before the tribulation begins. John 14:2-3 has been used to say that Christians will be taken to heaven by Christ before the time of great distress or tribulation is taking place on earth.

But you will see that these two verses do NOT support the secret rapture theory. It should be pointed out that these two verses are the only Words of Christ used to support the view that all Christians dead or alive will be gathered together and taken to heaven before the tribulation.

The other scriptures primarily used to support this view are the words of Paul in his letters to the Churches at Corinth and at Thessalonica, as you will see later. This chapter will not deal with the WHEN of a secret escape to heaven, which is not possible, but quite simply to show that NO MAN CAN GO TO THE PRESENT HEAVEN.

John 14:2 (KJV) In my Father's house are many mansions: if it were not so, I would have told you. I go to prepare a place for you. 3 And if I go and prepare a place for you, I will come again, and receive you unto myself; that where I am, there ye may be also

To fully understand these verses, it is necessary to study the context within which they are found. According to Nelson's New Illustrated Bible Dictionary 1995, "The primary rule of Biblical interpretation is 'context' ... let a passage speak for itself within the context of the paragraph, chapter, or book" (192).

In the Book of John, we find verses that answer the question, "Can man go to the present heaven?" The first answer to this question is found in a teaching Christ was giving to Nicodemus.

John 3:13 (NIV) No one has ever gone into heaven except the one who came from heaven- the Son of Man.

Another answer is found in John, chapters 13-17, which give an account of the evening of the Passover Feast which Christ spent with His disciples, just before He would be arrested. Everything in chapters 13-17 of John is one teaching, given at one time, to one audience, His disciples. In chapter 13, Jesus is telling His disciples that they **can not go** where He is going, back to His Father, in heaven.

John 13:33 (KJV) Little children, yet a little while I am with you. Ye shall seek me: and as I said unto the Jews, Whither I go, ye cannot come; ...

John 13:36 (KJV) Simon Peter said unto him, Lord, whither goest thou? Jesus answered him, Whither I go, thou canst not follow me now; but thou shalt follow me afterwards.

Jesus had been teaching that man can not go to heaven, but that born-again believers would enter into the "kingdom of heaven" also called the "kingdom of God". At the end of time, God is going to change his abode and live in the New Jerusalem. That is where you want to be, where God is.

Peter repeated what he had learned from Jesus when he told the crowd at the day of Pentecost:

Acts 2:34 (NIV) For David did not ascend to heaven, ...

So Jesus had already established the fact that man cannot go to the present heaven, where God is now. With this fact in mind, let's examine those verses, John 14:2-3 and see what Jesus was telling his disciples.

John 14:2 (KJV) In my Father's house are many mansions: if it were not so, I would have told you. I go to prepare a place for you. 3 And if I go and prepare a place for you, I will come again, and receive you unto myself; that where I am, there ye may be also.

The **place Jesus** is preparing for his followers is the new Jerusalem revealed here:

Revelation 21:1 (KJV) And I saw a new heaven and a new earth: for the first heaven and the first earth were passed away; and there was no more sea. 2 And I John saw the holy city, new Jerusalem, coming down from God out of heaven, prepared as a bride adorned for her husband. 3 And I heard a great voice out of heaven saying, Behold, the tabernacle of God is with men, and he will dwell with them, and they shall be his people, and God himself shall be with them, and be their God.

Millions of Christians who have been led to believe they will be taken off to heaven before the tribulation begins have in their possession a copy of the Life Application Bible, where we find:

"The New Jerusalem is where God lives among his people. Instead of our going up to meet him, he comes down to be with us ... " (2331).

The key to understanding what Jesus was telling his disciples in John 14:2-3 is found in the following verses:

John 14:4 And whither I go ye know, and the way ye know.

John 14:6 ... I am the way ...

John 14:12 ... I go unto my Father.

In verse 4, Jesus is telling his disciples two things. First, they know where He is going. He tells them in verse 12, to His Father .

Second, He tells them how they can also go to the Father, when He says, "and the way ye know". He defines "the way" in verse 6 when he says, "I am the way".

Jesus does not tell His disciples they can go to heaven.

No, Jesus is telling them "where He is going": "to His Father".

He also tells them He is the way to His Father, so that whoever believes in Him, can join Him and His Father in their new home, the New Jerusalem at a later time.

This is what He meant when He told Peter:

"thou shalt follow me afterwards." John 13:36.

Far too much emphasis has been placed on "going to heaven", which is only the temporary residence of God. Heaven will pass away as Jesus told us.

Matthew 24:35 " Heaven and earth shall pass away, but my words shall not pass away."

In ***John 13:36, Jesus said "Whither I go, thou canst not follow me now; but thou shalt follow me afterwards."*** Jesus is telling His disciples they cannot go to the present heaven, but will follow Him later into the New Jerusalem, so that *" **where I am, there ye may be also**"* of John 14:3 becomes true.

Jesus said His Words would not pass away. The Words in the Bible laying on the table are more permanent than the place that we call "heaven".

In John, chapters 13-17, in the King James Version, we find the word, "heaven", only once in John 17:1, where Christ "***lifted up his eyes to heaven***" and then prayed to His Father. The words "looked up into the sky" could be used without changing the meaning of the verse. Heaven is used here only to denote direction to His Father. However, in John, chapters 13-17, in the King James we find the word, **"Father"** used 50 times in 42 verses. **Jesus was teaching His disciples about "His Father", not about His temporary house, which we call heaven.**

The pre-tribulationists use Zechariah 14:5 to explain how the raptured believers return to earth from heaven. *Zechariah 14:5 (NIV) ... Then the LORD my God will come, and all the holy ones with him.*

The question "who are the 'holy ones' or 'saints' in the King James Version" is answered by Christ:

*Matthew 25:31 **When the Son of man shall come in his glory, and all the holy angels with him, then shall he sit upon the throne of his glory**... Matthew 16:27 For the Son of man shall come in the glory of his Father with his angels; and then he shall reward every man according to his works.*

So Jesus said that He would return with His angels. The Apostle Paul agrees that Jesus will bring with Him his **angels** when He returns.

2 Thessalonians 1:7 And to you who are troubled rest with us, when the Lord Jesus shall be revealed from heaven with his mighty angels,

So Christ will come again with his angels, not previously raptured believers. The pre-tribulation rapture theory through misuse of John 14:2-3, as you have just seen, presents a way to get believers to heaven, but then after the seven years in heaven have passed, it is necessary to get them back to earth. Because no verses can be found in the New Testament to support a return ticket from heaven to earth, it was necessary to go to this verse, Zechariah 14:5 in the King James, and twist it into the return ticket.

Zechariah 14:5 ... and the LORD my God shall come, and all the saints with thee.

The pre-tribulation rapture theory states that these **saints** are the previously raptured believers returning from heaven with Christ. Paul defines who these "saints" are Not, in his first letter to the believers in the church at Thessolonica:

1 Thessalonians 3:13 To the end he may stablish your hearts unblameable in holiness before God, even our Father, at the coming of our Lord Jesus Christ with all his saints.

Paul is telling the believers that he hopes God will strengthen their faith and actions so that they will be found without blame when Christ returns. If the "saints" accompanying Christ at his return were previously raptured believers, this sentence would make no sense, because those same believers that Paul is writing to would be returning with Christ. No, the saints are the angels accompanying Christ from heaven. This was previously shown in Matt 25:31 before.

Two important components of the pre-tribulation rapture theory cannot be supported by the Bible. First, God never intended for man to go to the present heaven. Second, there are no verses to support how man gets back to earth.

Let's now look at the third: the journey from earth to heaven. The pre-tribulation rapture theory teaches that First Thessalonians 4:13-18 gives the most detailed, comprehensive account of the rapture of the church in the Bible. Let's re-examine this passage of scripture:

1 Thessalonians 4:13(NIV) Brothers, we do not want you to be ignorant about those who fall asleep, or to grieve like the rest of men, who have no hope.14 We believe that Jesus died and rose again and so we believe that God will bring with Jesus those who have fallen asleep in him. 15 According to the Lord's own word, we tell you that we who are still alive, who are left till the coming of the Lord, will certainly not precede those who have fallen asleep. 16 For the Lord himself will come down from heaven, with a loud command, with the voice of the archangel and with the trumpet call of God, and the dead in Christ will rise first. 17 After that, we who are still alive and are left will be caught up together with them in the clouds to meet the Lord in the air. And so we will be with the Lord forever. 18 Therefore encourage each other with these words

In the Wuest Expanded Translation of The New Testament, 1 Thessalonians 4:16-17 is described as "a welcome-meeting with the Lord in the lower atmosphere.".

This will be a meeting in the air above earth with Jesus Christ when He returns with his angels to greet His followers both alive and asleep in the grave. Then they will be taken by Christ and his angels into the eternal state and finally into the New Jerusalem. The resurrection of the dead is described in :

Ezekiel 37:12 Therefore prophesy and say unto them, Thus saith the Lord GOD; Behold, O my people, I will open your graves, and cause you to come up out of your graves, and bring you into the land of Israel. 13 And ye shall know that I am the LORD, when I have opened your graves, O my people, and brought you up out of your graves, 14 And shall put my spirit in you, and ye shall live, and I shall place you in your own land: then shall ye know that I the LORD have spoken it, and performed it, saith the LORD.

The resurrection of the living is found in:

Ezekiel 37:21 And say unto them, Thus saith the Lord GOD; Behold, I will take the children of Israel from among the heathen, whither they be gone, and will gather them on every side, and bring them into their own land: 23 ... but I will save them out of all their dwelling places, wherein they have sinned, and will cleanse them: so shall they be my people, and I will be their God. 24 And David my servant shall be king over them; and they all shall have one shepherd: they shall also walk in my judgments, and observe my statutes, and do them.

Notice, God said He would cleanse them and put David, which is a reference to Christ, as King over them.

Some scholars would argue that the verses in Ezekiel above do not apply to the church, because he was talking to the Jews, not the church. Paul settled this debate when he said:

Ephesians 2:11-13(NIV) Therefore, remember that formerly you who are Gentiles by birth ...remember that at that time you were separate from Christ, excluded from citizenship in Israel and foreigners to the covenants of the promise, without hope and without God in the world. But now in Christ Jesus you who once were far away have been brought near through the blood of Christ. Ephesians 3:6(NIV) ... through the gospel the Gentiles are heirs together with Israel, members together of one body, and sharers together in the promise in Christ Jesus.

Therefore, if you have any hope of eternal life with Christ Jesus, your hope is that you have citizenship in Israel and that you "have been grafted in among the others" (Romans 11:17). Israel, in the Old Testament, was God's chosen people. Israel, in the New Testament, is still God's chosen people. The big difference is that ever since Christ died on the cross, God's chosen people are chosen because they have put their faith, hope and trust in Jesus Christ. The only blood that makes any difference now is the blood of Christ, Not a bloodline that may or may not be traced back to Israel.

Whenever, you encounter the Jehovah's Witnesses and they are trying to convert you, go straight to the heart of the matter and ask them, **"Who do you say Jesus is?"** They will avoid answering the question. But if you say, "Don't you believe that Jesus Christ is Michael, the archangel?", you can get them to confess that they do. Since born-again Christians believe that Jesus Christ is God in human flesh, you have nothing in common with the Jehovah's Witness. Once you explain this to them, they will soon leave.

The point is, the one and only GOD, creator of heaven and earth and everything in it, visited planet earth almost 2000 years ago in a body that has come to be known as Jesus. There are many other arguments that can be used by the Jehovah's Witnesses, but since they do not believe that Jesus Christ is God, the rest of their beliefs fall to the ground. The same is true with our discussion about the theory of believers going to heaven before the tribulation begins.

The heart of the matter is, Jesus, the one who will resurrect us, has told us **we cannot go where He is now, the present heaven.** But, we will follow Him later into the New Jerusalem, just as He told

Peter in John 13:36. **Therefore, the theory that believers will be taken to the present heaven, before the tribulation begins, falls to the ground.**

John 14:2-3 does not say Jesus will return and take His followers to heaven. No, it says His followers will spend eternity with Him. Where will He be? He will be in the new Jerusalem.

What Jesus Taught

4

The pre-tribulation theory teaches that Christ is going to come in the clouds and take all His followers to heaven before the tribulation. Its Biblical basis comes mainly from the letters of the Apostle Paul. As we discussed in the previous chapter, the only verses that Jesus spoke that this theory uses to support its teachings are found in John 14:2-3. But as you saw in the previous chapter, this is not accurately reporting what Jesus said. Jesus NEVER said He would come back and take His followers to heaven. No, He said that they would be with Him. The place Jesus was going to prepare for His followers is the New Jerusalem.

Many say that 1 Thessalonians 4:13-18, is the clearest teaching in all of the New Testament concerning the rapture of the church before the tribulation. We have already studied in detail this teaching about Christ coming again and found that Paul was telling the church at Thessalonica about the return of Christ. He explained to them, that Christ would come back for them, on the "day of the Lord". He told them not to be deceived, that the "day of the Lord", when Christ returns for them, will not come until **after** the man of lawlessness, the Antichrist, is revealed. However, what Christ had to say about this subject is important also because Paul tells us he received his message from the Lord.

1 Thessalonians 4:15 (KJV) "For this we say unto you by the word of the Lord".

So why not go straight to the source, the Lord Jesus Christ, and learn what he said about the resurrection. The following is perhaps, the clearest, most concise teaching showing that Jesus will condemn unbelievers at the same time he resurrects his believers, NOT seven years apart. This teaching by Christ, takes place at the death of his friend Lazarus. Jesus was talking to Martha, sister of Lazarus. Lazarus had already been dead for 4 days.

John 11:23-27 (NIV) Jesus said to her, "Your brother will rise again." Martha answered, "I know he will rise again in the resurrection at the last day." Jesus said to her, "I am the resurrection and the life. He who believes in me will live, even though he dies; and whoever lives and believes in me will never die. Do you believe this?" "Yes, Lord," she told him, "I believe that you are the Christ, the Son of God, who was to come into the world."

Jesus had previously taught Martha He would resurrect believers at the last day. How else would she have known?

Was Lazarus a believer? Yes, he was a friend of Jesus (John 11:11) and he as well as Martha and Mary were loved by Christ (John 11:5). What is the "**last day**"? Christ defines "the last day" in the book of John as follows:

John 6:39-40 (NIV) "And this is the will of him who sent me, that I shall lose none of all that he has given me, but raise them up at the last day. For my Father's will is that everyone who looks to the Son and believes in him shall have eternal life, and I will raise him up at the last day."

John 12:48 (NIV) There is a judge for the one who rejects me and does not accept my words; that very word which I spoke will condemn him at the last day.

Jesus will resurrect or raise up His believers at the **last day**. Jesus also will judge those who do not believe in Him **at the last day**. *It is one time for both believers and unbelievers*. Believers will be resurrected to life and unbelievers will be judged at the same time, at "the **last day**".

Holman Bible Handbook 1992 defines "last day": "The 'last day' (singular), however refers to the consummation of time and history when the great resurrection and judgment will occur of all persons (1 John 2:18)" (623).

Another example of Christ's teachings which plainly shows that

His followers and unbelievers will be resurrected at the same time, at the same hour, just as above, is also found in the gospel of John. In this teaching, Jesus is telling the Jews:

John 5:28-29 (KJV) ... for the hour is coming, in the which all that are in the graves shall hear his voice, and shall come forth; they that have done good, unto the resurrection of life; and they that have done evil, unto the resurrection of damnation.

"For the hour is coming" means at an instant, not a long period of time. "In the which" means within that instant. "All that are in the graves" means all that have died, both good and bad. Here, in the gospel of John above, chapter 5, we find another teaching that Jesus will resurrect all that have died, the godly and the ungodly at the same time. Looking at these same verses, John 5:28-29, in the <u>Wuest Expanded Translation</u>, we find:

Stop marveling at this, because there comes an hour in which all who are in the tombs shall hear His voice and shall come out, those who did the good things to a resurrection of life, those who practiced the evil things, to a resurrection of judgment.

"there comes an hour in which all who are in the tombs", teaches that the resurrection of the dead, both good and bad, is one event, at the same time.

Dr. Ray Summers was professor of New Testament interpretation at Southern Baptist Theological Seminary in Louisville from 1959 to 1964. In the fall of 1964 he moved to Baylor University, where he was Chairman of the Religion Department. In his book, <u>Worthy Is The Lamb</u>, he writes:

"When the entire New Testament is studied, it teaches one general resurrection (of both good and evil) and one general judgment (of both good and evil), both of which are directly related to the second coming of Christ which brings to an end this world order and ushers in the eternal heavenly order" (206).

Dr. Summers, truly a Bible scholar, also authored <u>Essentials of New Testament Greek</u> used in seminaries today.

The Old Testament book of Daniel agrees with a resurrection of the just and the unjust at the same time.

"At that time Michael, the great prince who protects your people, will

arise. There will be a time of distress such as has not happened from the beginning of nations until then. But at that time your people--everyone whose name is found written in the book--will be delivered. Multitudes who sleep in the dust of the earth will awake: some to everlasting life, others to shame and everlasting contempt". Daniel 12:1-2 (NIV)

The "book" is the "book of life" mentioned in: *Revelation 20:15(KJV) And whosoever was not found written in the book of life was cast into the lake of fire.*

"Your people– everyone whose name is found written in the book" in Daniel 12 above includes everyone who will spend eternity with Christ. Don't try to say "he was just talking about the Jews". If a Gentile's name is not found in the book he will be "cast into the lake of fire". Remember, Paul said in Romans 10:12 there is no difference between Jew and Gentile.

The Apostle Paul agrees with Jesus, that **the resurrection of the dead, both good and bad, is one event, at the same time**, in both his letters to the Church of the Thessalonians. In 1 Thessalonians 5:1-5:5, Paul told the brothers, the church, that *"the day of the Lord"* will come like a "thief in the night".

Paul wrote and told them not to be surprised when this day comes and brings sudden destruction on the heathen. Because Paul did not know when Christ would come back, he wrote to them as though it could happen very soon and they could be alive to witness *"the day of the Lord"*.

If they did live to see that day, it would not surprise them, because he had warned them to keep watch. If there was to be a rapture or a "taking away" of believers prior to the *"day of the Lord"*, there would be no need to warn the brothers about the *"day of the Lord"* bringing destruction. The brothers would have already left the earth.

In 2 Thessalonians 1:4-10, Paul told the church that Christ will give them relief from persecution when he comes back to punish the ungodly. Both events happen at the same time for believers and unbelievers at the end of the tribulation period. There are no discrepancies in this Holy Book. The Apostle Peter warned us about those that would distort Paul's letters.

2 Peter 3:15-16 (NIV) Bear in mind that our Lord's patience means salvation, just as our dear brother Paul also wrote you with the wisdom that

God gave him. He writes the same way in all his letters, speaking in them of these matters. His letters contain some things that <u>are hard to understand, which ignorant and unstable people distort, as they do the other Scriptures, to their own destruction.</u>

We have discussed the resurrection of the dead, but "what about those believers that are still alive?" The Apostle Paul tells us they will not precede those that have fallen asleep (dead).

1 Thessalonians 4:15 (NIV) According to the Lord's own word, we tell you that we who are still alive, who are left till the coming of the Lord, will certainly not precede those who have fallen asleep.

We have already established that the resurrection of the dead, those asleep, whether just or unjust will occur at the same time. After that, the living believers will be caught up to meet Christ in the air.

There will Not be a secret snatching away of believers seven years before Christ returns.

Let's now focus on what Jesus had to say about "the end of the age". First, let's look at the parable of the weeds.

Matthew 13:24-30 *Another parable put he forth unto them, saying, The kingdom of heaven is likened unto a man which sowed good seed in his field: But while men slept, his enemy came and sowed tares among the wheat, and went his way. But when the blade was sprung up, and brought forth fruit, then appeared the tares also. So the servants of the householder came and said unto him, Sir, didst not thou sow good seed in thy field? from whence then hath it tares? He said unto them, An enemy hath done this. The servants said unto him, Wilt thou then that we go and gather them up? But he said, Nay; lest while ye gather up the tares, ye root up also the wheat with them. Let both grow together until the harvest: and in the time of harvest I will say to the reapers, Gather ye together first the tares, and bind them in bundles to burn them: but gather the wheat into my barn.*

Let's look at the explanation Jesus gave.

Matthew 13:37-43 (TNIV) *He answered, "The one who sowed the good seed is the Son of Man. The field is the world, and the good seed stands for the people of the kingdom. The weeds are the people of the evil one, and the enemy who sows them is the devil. The harvest is the end of the age, and the harvesters are angels. "As the weeds are pulled up and burned in the fire, so it will be at the end of the age. The Son of Man will send out his angels, and they will weed out of his kingdom everything that causes sin and all who do evil. They will throw them into the blazing furnace, where there will be weeping and gnashing of teeth. Then the righteous will shine like the sun in the kingdom of their Father. Whoever has ears, let them hear.*

This passage clearly indicates that the tares or sinners will be harvested first and burned. This contradicts the teaching of Christians escaping to heaven, first. The ones taken are not being "raptured", rather they are being "weeded out" and then burned.

Matthew 24 :40-41 (NIV) Two men will be in the field; one will be taken and the other left. Two women will be grinding with a hand mill; one will be taken and the other left.

<u>Luke explains very clearly what happens to those that are taken.</u>

Luke 17:34 -37 (NIV) I tell you, on that night two people will be in one bed; one will be taken and the other left. Two women will be grinding grain together; one will be taken and the other left. " Where, Lord?" they asked. He replied, "Where there is a dead body, there the vultures will gather."

The King James used "eagles" instead of vultures . The eagle was a symbol of God's judgment in the Old Testament (Jeremiah 48:40; Ezekiel 17:3,7).

Job 39:27-30 (NIV) *"Does the eagle soar at your command and build his nest on high? ..., His young ones feast on blood, and where the slain are, there is he."*

Revelation 19:17 (NIV) *And I saw an angel standing in the sun, who cried in a loud voice to all the birds flying in midair, "Come, gather together for the great supper of God, This is God's wrath upon the wicked where the great birds will feast upon the flesh of the wicked."*

<u>You do not want to be the one taken. You want to be left behind.</u>

Look at Matthew 24:37-39 (NIV) *As it was in the days of Noah, so it will be at the coming of the Son of Man. For in the days before the flood, people were eating and drinking, marrying and giving in marriage, up to the day Noah entered the ark; and they knew nothing about what would happen until the flood came and took them all away. That is how it will be at the coming of the Son of Man.*

This is often quoted to show that the rapture could not come after the tribulation begins because they say Jesus is describing a peaceful time. But Jesus was talking about the sin in the world.

Genesis 6:11 (NIV) *Now the earth was corrupt in God's sight and was full of violence*. Yes, Satan's business (sin) will still be going on, as usual, when Jesus returns just like it was when Noah entered the ark. The "parable of the net" gives us a clear understanding of what will take place at the "end of the age".

Matthew 13:47 -51 (NIV) *"Once again, the kingdom of heaven is like a net that was let down into the lake and caught all kinds of fish. When it was full, the fishermen pulled it up on the shore. Then they sat down and collected the good fish in baskets, but threw the bad away. <u>This is how it will be at the end of the age. The angels will come and separate the wicked from the righteous and throw them into the fiery furnace, where there will be weeping and gnashing of teeth.</u> "Have you understood all these things?" Jesus asked. "Yes," they replied.*

These parables of Jesus are not just for Jews that missed the rapture, as some would say. No, Jesus is talking to you because you will still be here.

Christ taught that He would resurrect the dead, good and bad, at the same time, at the last day, also called, the "day of the Lord". At that time, He will reward His believers and punish the wicked and unbelievers.

When We Put on Immortality

5

We will do as the Apostle Paul commanded: *Prove all things; hold fast that which is good. 1 Thessalonians 5:21.*

Verses 1 Corinthians 15:51-52 are used as one of the principal Bible references to substantiate the secret snatching away of the bride of Christ before the tribulation begins.

Once again, why is it important to know that God does not have an escape planned?

Because Jesus warned us that when persecution comes because of the Word, many will fall away, but if you endure till the end, you will be saved. (Matt. 24:13).

It is time for the Church to start preaching perseverance, not prosperity. God has already given us prosperity, what did we do with it?

Let's take a close look at 1 Corinthians 15:51-52 in relation to the other writings of Paul and their context within the book and chapter where they are found.

Paul is writing to the Church in Corinth. In 1 Corinthians chapter 15, Paul is discussing the resurrection of the dead in his letter to the brethren at Corinth. Paul tells the brethren the order in which the resurrections will occur. First, Christ was resurrected, then when he comes again, he will resurrect those that belong to Him, dead or alive. Then in verses 51 and 52 below he tells them a mystery, something they haven't heard before, which is, all believers, dead or alive, will receive a new imperishable body. Once this begins to happen, it will happen very quickly, when the last trumpet blows. We are not questioning whether this will happen. We know, with certainty, we, the believers in Christ, will receive a new immortal body, when Christ returns. What we need to do is investigate WHEN this will happen in relation to the tribulation and the appearance of the Antichrist.

1 Corinthians 15:23 But every man in his own order: Christ the firstfruits; afterward they that are Christ's at his coming. 24 Then cometh the end, when he shall have delivered up the kingdom to God, even the Father; when he shall have put down all rule and all authority and power. 25 For he must reign, till he hath put <u>all enemies</u> under his feet. 26 <u>The last enemy that shall be destroyed is death</u>.

51 Behold, I shew you a mystery; We shall not all sleep, but we shall all be changed,

52 In a moment, in the twinkling of an eye, at the last trump: for the trumpet shall sound, and the dead shall be raised incorruptible, and we shall be changed. 53 For this corruptible must put on incorruption, and this mortal must put on immortality. 54 So when this corruptible shall have put on incorruption, and this mortal shall have put on immortality, then shall be brought to pass the saying that is written, Death is swallowed up in victory.

Paul is saying that when Christ comes back: He must reign and destroy all His enemies, which includes Satan and his angels. Verse 26 tells us that the last enemy to be destroyed is death. Paul is telling us that Christ will destroy Satan and his angels, included in the group, "all enemies", when He returns to give us our new immortal bodies. Christ is not going to do this twice: once before the tribulation and then again at the end. No, we will only receive our new immortal bodies at the end of the tribulation. In verse 54 above, Paul is quoting:

Isaiah 25:8 He will swallow up death in victory; and the Lord GOD will wipe away tears from off all faces; and the rebuke of his people shall he take away from off all the earth: for the LORD hath spoken it.

Let's examine Isaiah so we can understand the setting surrounding this glorious feat of God. To put Isaiah 25:8 in its proper context we need to start at Isaiah chapter 24.

Isaiah chapters 24:1-27:13 is referred to as "Prophecies of the Day of the Lord", according to <u>Nelson's Illustrated Bible Dictionary 1992</u>, (607).

Remember: Paul said Christ would gather up His believers on

"the day of the Lord" (1 Thess. 4:16-5:4).

Isaiah 24:1 (NIV) See, the LORD is going to lay waste the earth and devastate it; he will ruin its face and scatter its inhabitants– 5 The earth is defiled by its people; they have disobeyed the laws, violated the statutes and broken the everlasting covenant. 21 In that day the LORD will punish the powers in the heavens above and the kings on the earth below. 23 The moon will be abashed, the sun ashamed; for the LORD Almighty will reign on Mount Zion and in Jerusalem, and before its elders, gloriously.

Isaiah 25:6(NIV) On this mountain the LORD Almighty will prepare a feast of rich food for all peoples, a banquet of aged wine-- the best of meats and the finest of wines. 7 On this mountain he will destroy the shroud that enfolds all peoples, the sheet that covers all nations; 8 he will swallow up death forever. The Sovereign LORD will wipe away the tears from all faces; he will remove the disgrace of his people from all the earth. The LORD has spoken. 9 In that day they will say, "Surely this is our God; we trusted in him, and he saved us. This is the LORD, we trusted in him; let us rejoice and be glad in his salvation." 10 The hand of the LORD will rest on this mountain;

Isaiah 26:19 (NIV) But your dead will live; their bodies will rise. You who dwell in the dust, wake up and shout for joy. Your dew is like the dew of the morning; the earth will give birth to her dead. 20 Go, my people, enter your rooms and shut the doors behind you; hide yourselves for a little while until his wrath has passed by. 21 See, the LORD is coming out of his dwelling to punish the people of the earth for their sins. The earth will disclose the blood shed upon her; she will conceal her slain no longer.

Isaiah is saying that BEFORE death is swallowed up, God is going to punish the wicked. He is going to come and reign on Mount Zion and in Jerusalem. On Mountain Zion during His great feast, He will remove the shroud that covers us. He will eliminate death. He will wipe away all of our tears. He will remove all our disgrace. He strongly confirms this with the words, "The LORD has spoken" (Is. 25:8). In Isaiah 26:19 he tells us the dead will be resurrected. In verse 20 and 21 he tells us to go into our houses, shut the door, and wait while His wrath is poured out on the wicked.

The clue that this prophecy pertains to the "day of the Lord", when Jesus will return, is given in Isaiah 24:23, where he tells us the sun and moon will not give any light. This is the sign that the "day of the Lord" is here. It is repeated in:

Joel 2:31 (NIV) The sun will be turned to darkness and the moon to blood before the coming of the great and dreadful day of the LORD.

Mark 13:24 (NIV) "But in those days, following that distress, "'the sun will be darkened, and the moon will not give its light;

Acts 2:20 (NIV) The sun will be turned to darkness and the moon to blood before the coming of the great and glorious day of the Lord.

Another point that needs to be made is that God is going to wipe away all our tears (Is 25:8). The following verses tell us WHEN God will do this. The following is an example of John getting a glimpse into the new Jerusalem, as he described in the Book of Revelation. Notice in verse 17, that here, in the new Jerusalem, God will wipe away the tears. It does not happen, in the air, or on the way to the present heaven, or in the present heaven while the tribulation is going on.

Revelation 7:9 (KJV) After this I beheld, and, lo, a great multitude, which no man could number, of all nations, and kindreds, and people, and tongues, stood before the throne, and before the Lamb, clothed with white robes, and palms in their hands; 13 And one of the elders answered, saying unto me, What are these which are arrayed in white robes? and whence came they? 14 And I said unto him, Sir, thou knowest. And he said to me, These are they which came out of great tribulation, and have washed their robes, and made them white in the blood of the Lamb. 15 Therefore are they before the throne of God, and serve him day and night in his temple: and he that sitteth on the throne shall dwell among them. 16 They shall hunger no more, neither thirst any more; neither shall the sun light on them, nor any heat. 17 For the Lamb which is in the midst of the throne shall feed them, and shall lead them unto living fountains of waters: and <u>God shall wipe away all tears from their eyes.</u>

John tells us again WHEN God will wipe away our tears.

Revelation 21:1-4 (KJV) And I saw a new heaven and a new earth: for the first heaven and the first earth were passed away; and there was no more sea. And I John saw the holy city, new Jerusalem, coming down from God out of heaven, prepared as a bride adorned for her husband. And I heard a great voice out of heaven saying, Behold, the tabernacle of God is with men, and he will dwell with them, and *they shall be his people, and God himself shall be with them, and be their God. And <u>God shall wipe away all tears from their eyes; and there shall be no more death,</u> neither sorrow, nor crying, neither shall there be any more pain: for the former things are passed away.*

God will wipe away our tears and abolish death when we are brought into our new eternal home, the new Jerusalem. Then Christ's promise, *that where I am, there ye may be also* in John 14:3 comes true.

Using 1 Corinthians 15:51-52 to support a theory that Christ is going to come back and take His followers to heaven before the tribulation, is distorting what Paul was writing.

After our thorough analysis you can see that we will get our new immortal bodies only after Christ returns and destroys death. Remember in 1 Corinthians 15:26 Paul told us the last enemy Christ destroys is death. If there will be a rapture before the tribulation, then Christ will have to snatch up His followers, give them immortality which destroys death for them only, before the Antichrist is revealed and the period of the tribulation begins. Then Christ would have to do it again at His second coming which is at the end of the tribulation. The Bible tells us in Revelation 13 that those who refuse to worship the image of the beast will be killed. In the midst of the tribulation, from heaven we hear:

Revelation 14:13 (NIV) Then I heard a voice from heaven say, "Write: Blessed are the dead who die in the Lord from now on."

Death cannot possibly be destroyed before the martyrs of the tribulation die.

Christ is not going to destroy death more than once. If all believers in Christ exit the earth before the tribulation, then who are the tribulation martyrs? You will see in a later chapter that no one gets saved during the tribulation, therefore the martyrs were Christians before the tribulation began. This demonstrates yet another flaw in the theory of the pre-tribulation rapture.

Paul had been teaching his brothers, at the church of Corinth, that Christ would come back for them on the "day of the Lord". Examples of this are found in the following verses.

In the following scripture, Paul was teaching about what to do with a member of the church that was openly living with his father's wife. Paul is telling the Church to expel the wicked brother from the Church and hopefully this will lead to repentance so that his soul will be saved on the **"day of the Lord"**.

1 Corinthians 5:5 (NIV) hand this man over to Satan, so that the sinful nature may be destroyed and his spirit saved on the day of the Lord.

Paul always taught that the reward for believers would come on "the day of the Lord". The second example illustrating this truth is:

2 Corinthians 1:13-14 (NIV) .... And I hope that, as you have understood us in part, you will come to understand fully that you can boast of us just as we will boast of you in the day of the Lord Jesus.

Please don't try to make a difference between "day of the Lord", "day of Christ" or "day of the Lord Jesus" used in the preceding verse. Paul is talking about the same event in all of these. In John 10:30, Jesus said "I and the Father are one".

You will notice that sometimes we say Jesus, at other times, Jesus Christ, and then at times Christ, but we are always talking about our Lord and Savior Jesus Christ. Jesus, Jesus Christ, Christ, Lord Jesus, and Lord Jesus Christ are all names of our GOD.

Our Lord Jesus Christ is going to come back at the end of the tribulation to reward His followers and to judge the sinners all at the same time. God's plan is not as complicated as the made-up plan that needs charts to outline future events such as Christ coming back twice; once to rapture the church and then seven years later in judgment.

Two verses, 1 Corinthians 15:51 and 52, have been taken out of context and used to say something entirely different than what Paul, the writer, is trying to convey.

First Corinthians 15:51-52 and 1 Thessalonians 4:13-18, thoroughly examined in chapter 1, are two of the most important scripture references used by those who say that Christians will be taken to heaven before the tribulation. Paul was very clear that death was the last enemy Christ will destroy when He comes again.

Cyrus I. Scofield, author of the well distributed Scofield Reference Bible, agrees with this: "but death, the "last enemy" (1 Cor. 15.26),

WHEN WE PUT ON IMMORTALITY • 41

is not destroyed till after Satan's rebellion at the end of the thousand years" (769).

How is this possible when Scofield claims that believers "shall be raised incorruptible ..." (1 Corinthians 15:52) before the tribulation? (1227-8).

Scofield claims there will be a resurrection unto life, which will destroy death, before the tribulation and then claims death won't be destroyed until after the millennial reign.

Just as Paul commanded, we have tested the theory of a rapture before the tribulation and it has failed the test. We do not receive our new immortal bodies until after the tribulation, not seven years earlier as this theory teaches. Therefore, this teaching is Not something we will hold on to. ... *Thou art weighed in the balances, and art found wanting. Daniel 5:27.*

God will wipe away our tears and abolish death when we are brought into our new eternal home, the New Jerusalem. Then Christ's promise, "that where I am, there ye may be also" in John 14:3 comes true. Paul told us the last enemy Christ destroys is death. (1 Corinthians 15:26).

If there will be a rapture before the tribulation, Christ would have to give His followers their immortal bodies at that time, which destroys death. Then, at His second coming after the tribulation, Christ would have to destroy death the second time. No, this is not His plan.

Absent From Body, Present With The Lord

6

During a recent funeral service, the pastor, in speaking about a departed brother in Christ, made reference to the often heard verse: *We are confident, I say, and willing rather to be absent from the body, and to be present with the Lord (2 Corinthians 5:8).*

The pastor said "Take comfort because our beloved brother Sam is now with the Lord, because the Bible says that to be absent from the body is to be present with the Lord". This is often spoken in times of sorrow in regards to a departed loved one. The inference is that Sam is now in the presence of Jesus. But we need to examine the text to see if this is really what the Apostle Paul was saying. Lets go back and put this verse into its context.

2 Corinthians 5:1 For we know that if our earthly house of this tabernacle were dissolved, we have a building of God, an house not made with hands, eternal in the heavens. 2 For in this we groan, earnestly desiring to be clothed upon with <u>our house which is from heaven:</u> 3 If so be that being clothed we shall not be found naked. 4 For we that are in this tabernacle do groan, being burdened: not for that we would be unclothed, but clothed upon, that mortality might be swallowed up of life. 5 Now he that hath wrought us for the selfsame thing is God, who also hath given unto us the earnest of the Spirit. 6 Therefore we are always confident, knowing that, whilst we are at home in the body, we are absent from the Lord: 7 (For we walk by faith, not by sight:) 8 We are confident, I say, and willing rather to be absent from the body, and to be present with the Lord.

Paul is saying that we have an eternal body which is in heaven. He is saying that we can not receive that eternal body while we are still

• 43

in this mortal body. He goes on to say that as long as we are in this mortal body we are away from God and that we long to be present with God. Paul also says that we must leave this life in order to enter into the next life where we will be present with the Lord. Paul is NOT saying that as soon as we leave this life we enter into the next. To do so would mean he would be contradicting what he had just told the Church in Corinth previously in the beginning of this letter.

.... And I hope that, as you have understood us in part, you will come to understand fully that you can boast of us just as we will boast of you in the day of the Lord Jesus. 2 Corinthians 1:13-14 (NIV)

Paul has just told the church that he would boast of their salvation in the "day of the Lord".

If they went directly to be with Jesus at their death, this verse would make no sense. All the members of that church would have been with Jesus about 1900 years by now. But we are still waiting for the "day of the Lord". So the time when Paul will boast of the Church at Corinth is still in the future. Where are these Church members now? We will let Jesus answer the question.

John 5:28-29 (KJV) ... for the hour is coming, in the which <u>all that are in the graves</u> shall hear his voice, and shall come forth; they that have done good, unto the resurrection of life; and they that have done evil, unto the resurrection of damnation.

All of the dead are waiting in their graves for Jesus to give the command. Those who have known Jesus as their Lord and Savior will rise to receive their new immortal body and be ushered into an eternal life with Jesus. Those who have rejected Jesus will rise to spend an eternity in hell.

Notice Jesus said, *"the hour is coming, in the which"*, this means at one time, at one hour, Jesus will resurrect both the good and the bad and pass judgment on all. It will all happen at the same time.

Back to the funeral, Sam will not know, when he is awakened by Jesus, whether he has been asleep for one day or thousands of days. Right now, he is asleep in peace.

Let's revisit the following verse where Paul was telling the brothers about what to do with a member of the church that was openly living with his father's wife.

1 Corinthians 5:5 (NIV) hand this man over to Satan, so that the sinful nature may be destroyed and his spirit saved on the day of the Lord.

Paul is telling the Church to expel the wicked brother from the Church and this may lead to repentance so that his soul will be saved on the "day of the Lord". Remember, believers in Christ, those dead or alive, will enter into the eternal state with a new body when Christ returns for us on the "day of the Lord".

The survivors of a dearly departed believer in Christ can be comforted by the fact that their loved one is in a state of peaceful rest and will on the "<u>day of the Lord</u>" arise and receive their eternal bodies before the living receive their eternal bodies and then the scripture:

1 Thessalonians 4:15 For this we say unto you by the word of the Lord, that we which are <u>alive and remain unto the coming of the Lord shall not prevent them which are asleep</u>. 16 For the Lord himself shall descend from heaven with a shout, with the voice of the archangel, and with the trump of God: and the <u>dead in Christ shall rise first</u>: 17 <u>Then we which are alive and remain</u> shall be caught up together with them in the clouds, to meet the Lord in the air: and so shall we ever be with the Lord **comes true**.

<u>The real joy is knowing that your loved one will Not spend eternity in hell.</u>

When you look at what Paul was teaching about the two different bodies and put that in context with what he had been teaching about salvation occurring on the "day of the Lord" you can see that he never meant to imply that as soon as a believer dies he is instantly with Christ.

Our discussion would not be complete without an explanation of the thief on the cross.

Then he [thief] *said, "Jesus, remember me when you come into your kingdom. Jesus answered him, "I tell you the truth, today you will be with me in paradise." Luke 23:42-43 (NIV).*

Some say that the moment the thief died he was in heaven with Jesus. If this were true, it would contradict so many of the teachings that have already been discussed in great detail. No, Jesus was telling the thief that at the moment the thief said, *"Remember me when you come into your kingdom"* the thief's eternal destiny had changed and that he would live eternally with Christ in paradise.

Remember, the thief said, *"When you come into your kingdom"*. Right now, the thief is still in the ground with Sam and millions more peacefully awaiting the resurrection Paul talked about in 1 Thessalonians 4:13-5:4. When Christ returns on "the day of the Lord", the thief will be welcomed into the kingdom of Christ along with Sam and millions of other believers.

Back to Sam, the next conscience moment he will experience is when he comes into the presence of Jesus on the "day of the Lord". He will receive his new immortal body and see Jesus and live eternally in glory with Him. Hallelujah.

7 | What Does Billy Graham Believe

You have already seen conclusive proof that the world's number one evangelist of all time, the Apostle Paul, believed and wrote to the brethren, the members of the Churches that he had started, that they would be on earth to see the rise of the lawless one, the Antichrist (2 Thessalonians 2). Remember, Paul thought that the end of the earth, as we know it, would come during his lifetime.

Paul said in 1 Thessalonians 5:2-3 that the day when Christ returns, that is, the "day of the Lord", would come as a "thief in the night" and would mean "sudden destruction" to the unsaved. In the next verse, Paul tells the brethren that "the day", ["the day of the Lord'] would not be a surprise to them. So Paul was writing to the brethren fully expecting them to be on earth to witness Christ coming back in power and glory to destroy the unbelievers. Paul did not believe or write that the "great escape" for believers would occur before the tribulation begins.

Let's see if the number one evangelist of our time, Billy Graham, believes just as the Apostle Paul, that the Church will be on earth to witness the reign of the Antichrist. Billy Graham does not come out and say, "I do not believe in a pre-tribulation rapture of the Church".

However, passages from Billy Graham's book, <u>Storm Warning</u>, show us he is in total agreement with Paul that the Church will not be air lifted out before the tribulation begins.

Speaking of the book of Revelation, Billy Graham writes, "Revelation is a pastor's letter to his floundering flock, an urgent telegram bearing a brilliant battle plan for a people at war" (75).

Some defenders of the pre-tribulation rapture theory say the letters to the seven churches found in chapters 2 and 3 of the book of Revelation are addressed only to specific church eras, or time periods in church history. and that we are living in the last era, the church of Laodicea.

Graham refutes this with,"I do believe, ... that each vision is as important and as full of meaning and application today to you and me, as it was to those seven churches in Asia" (86).

So Graham tells us that we should heed the words of Christ to ALL the churches when he said *"He that hath an ear, let him hear what the Spirit saith unto the churches" (Revelation 2:29)*.

Graham goes on to mention that John, who was told by Christ to *"Write the things which thou hast seen"* (Revelation 1:11), was allowed to "see" the perils awaiting the Church. Here, Graham refers to John as the "seer".

Quoting Graham: "Had the seer been wondering if in fact there was sufficient power available to him and to his flock to withstand the dangers of that evil day, ..." (87).

The term "evil day" refers to the tribulation. Paul talked about it.

"Wherefore take unto you the whole armour of God, that ye may be able to withstand in the evil day, and having done all, to stand" (Ephesians 6:13).

There have been many fine sermons delivered about putting on the "whole armour of God". Paul was telling the brethren that they would need the "whole armour of God" to resist the devil during the tribulation, which Paul described as "the evil day". Day here is used in the singular, not in the plural as when Paul talked about all days being evil. *"Redeeming the time, because the days are evil" (Ephesians 5:16)*.

Therefore, "the evil day" is referring to the time when the devil has complete control of the earth or the time that we call "the tribulation".

Paul told us how to prepare for the evil day, the tribulation, in Ephesians chapter six.

11 Put on the whole armour of God, that ye may be able to stand

against the wiles of the devil.

12 For we wrestle not against flesh and blood, but against principalities, against powers, against the rulers of the darkness of this world, against spiritual wickedness in high places.

13 Wherefore take unto you the whole armour of God, that ye may be able to withstand in the evil day, and having done all, to stand.

14 Stand therefore, having your loins girt about with truth, and having on the breastplate of righteousness;

15 And your feet shod with the preparation of the gospel of peace;

16 Above all, taking the shield of faith, wherewith ye shall be able to quench all the fiery darts of the wicked.

17 And take the helmet of salvation, and the sword of the Spirit, which is the word of God:

18 Praying always with all prayer and supplication in the Spirit, and watching thereunto with all perseverance and supplication for all saints;

The most conclusive proof that Graham offers to prove that he believes the church will be on earth to face the devil during "the evil day", the tribulation, is his reference to the letters to the seven churches when Graham writes: "The letters are His words of power that will help us survive the evil day to come" (96).

Graham tells us very clearly that the Church will be on earth to witness the return of Christ after the tribulation according to Matthew 24:29 *"Immediately after the distress of those days ..."*.

Graham writes about that time, after the tribulation when Jesus will come back, and says: "The good news for Christians who have remained faithful through trials and persecution will be bad news indeed for everyone who has denied Christ,..." (38).

Graham provides more proof of his belief that the Church will soon be called upon to endure the time of the Antichrist and his rule on earth with the title of his book, Storm Warning. If Graham believed in a fly away before the storm hits, he might have called his book, "Escaping The Storm". No, Billy Graham is telling us to get prepared because the greatest storm of all times, the event called the tribulation is approaching.

You have seen proof that the world's two greatest evangelists, the Apostle Paul and Billy Graham do NOT believe Christians will exit the earth before the tribulation begins.

Jesus Gave Us a Sign

8

The most comprehensive account of the second coming of Christ in the Bible is given in Matthew chapter 24 and 25. It is also repeated in Mark 13 and Luke 21. It is that important.

Matthew 24:1 (KJV) And Jesus went out, and departed from the temple: and his disciples came to him for to show him the buildings of the temple.2 And Jesus said unto them, See ye not all these things? verily I say unto you, There shall not be left here one stone upon another, that shall not be thrown down.3 And as he sat upon the mount of Olives, the disciples came unto him privately, saying, Tell us, when shall these things be? and what shall be the sign of thy coming, and of the end of the world?

Note the disciples asked Christ three questions:

1. When will the temple be destroyed?
2. What will be the sign that He is returning?
3. What will be the sign of the end of the world?

We know that the temple in Jerusalem was destroyed in 70 A.D. by the Romans. The answer to the second question is found in Matthew 24:21-31. The answer to the last question is found in Matthew 24:4-14. These are the verses where the answers to the specific questions are found, however, Christ gave us much more information about events that would precede His coming again that He knew we needed to know. This information begins in verse 4 of chapter 24 and continues all the way through chapter 25.

First, those key verses will be examined that answer the second question: What will be the sign that He is returning?

Matthew 24:21 (KJV) For then shall be great tribulation, such as was not since the beginning of the world to this time, no, nor ever shall be. 24 For there shall arise false Christs, and false prophets, and shall show great signs and wonders; insomuch that, if it were possible, they shall deceive the very elect. 27 For as the lightning cometh out of the east, and shineth even unto the west; so shall also the coming of the Son of man be.

29 Immediately after the tribulation of those days shall the sun be darkened, and the moon shall not give her light, and the stars shall fall from heaven, and the powers of the heavens shall be shaken: 30 And then shall appear the sign of the Son of man in heaven: and then shall all the tribes of the earth mourn, and they shall see the Son of man coming in the clouds of heaven with power and great glory. 31 And he shall send his angels with a great sound of a trumpet, and they shall gather together his elect from the four winds, from one end of heaven to the other.

He tells them the sign to look for, to know for sure, that He is returning, is when the sun, moon and stars no longer shine. Why does He tell them this? Look at verse 24. He has already told them there would be false Christs performing miracles, but these impostors would not be the true Christ. He wanted them to know how to recognize Him from the impostors. He knew that the Antichrist would be on the world scene BEFORE He returned. He did not want His followers to be deceived into believing the Antichrist was Christ. Jesus has given us a sign so that we will know, without a doubt, that He is about to appear in the clouds with His great multitude of angels.

<u>When the sun, moon and stars grow dark is the sign that Jesus Christ is about to return.</u> Matthew 24:27 tells us when He returns the whole world will see it. It will not be secret. Jesus tells His disciples that He will return "Immediately after the tribulation of those days".

Darkness fell upon the earth at noon for three hours when Christ was crucified. (Matthew 27:45). His return will also be preceded by darkness.

As stated before, the answer to the last question, "What will be the sign of the end of the world?", is found in:

Matthew 24:4 (KJV) And Jesus answered and said unto them, Take heed that no man deceive you. 5 For many shall come in my name, saying, I am Christ; and shall deceive many. 6 And ye shall hear of wars and *rumours of wars: see that ye be not troubled: for all these things must come to pass, but the end is not yet. 7 For nation shall rise against nation, and kingdom against kingdom: and there shall be famines, and pestilences, and earthquakes, in divers places. 8 All these are the beginning of sorrows. 9 Then shall they deliver you up to be afflicted, and shall kill you: and ye shall be hated of all nations for my name's sake. 10 And then shall many be offended, and shall betray one another, and shall hate one another. 11 And many false prophets shall rise, and shall deceive many. 12 And because iniquity shall abound, the love of many shall wax cold. 13 But he that shall endure unto the end, the same shall be saved. **14 And this gospel of the kingdom shall be preached in all the world for a witness unto all nations; and then shall the end come.***

All of these verses (4-14) describe the coming of the end of the world. Note verse 11, carefully. Christ is warning that many false prophets will come with a message that does not line up with the Word of God. How do you know? You must carefully check to see if what the prophets say is supported by the complete teachings in the Bible. A premise backed up only by a verse or two taken out of context won't prove anything.

Jesus told His disciples everything that is recorded in Matthew chapters 24 and 25, Luke chapter 21 and Mark chapter 13 just two days before the Passover, three days before He was to die.

Matthew 26:1-2 (KJV) And it came to pass, when Jesus had finished all these sayings, he said unto his disciples, Ye know that after two days is the feast of the passover, and the Son of man is betrayed to be crucified.

"All these sayings" that Jesus had told His disciples are in chapters 24 and 25 of Matthew. Everything Jesus said in these two chapters was given as answers to the questions above. Note that Jesus had told his disciples all of this just two days before the Passover.

He mentioned that He would come again **after the tribulation** and gather all of His elect.

In the chapter of this book, "In my Father's House", it was stated that John 14:2-3 is used by the pre-tribulationists to say that Christ would take His followers to heaven before the tribulation begins.

Remember, the setting for John chapter 14 took place during the Passover meal. Christ was spending His last hours with His disciples before He would leave the earth and return to His Father. He was trying to prepare them for His departure.

Just two days before the Passover, Christ told His disciples that He would return after the tribulation. He gave them very lengthy answers to their questions as set forth above in Matthew chapters 24–25 of what would happen after He left them.

For the pre-tribulation rapture to be valid you must agree that two days after Jesus had told His disciples everything that is recorded in Matthew 24 and 25 and discussed above, He is now telling them they would escape earth before the tribulation and be taken to heaven. Can you believe that Christ would change His story so completely and so drastically in only two days? Teaching that Jesus will come and take the church to heaven before the tribulation using John 14:2-3 as a scriptural basis, is completely contrary to what Jesus was telling His disciples just two days earlier, as recorded in Matthew 24 and 25. Do you think Jesus would spend hours, telling His disciples about the trials and persecutions that would take place after He departed from the earth, and then two days later, say He was going to come for them secretly and take them to heaven? Of course not. If Christ had said this, it would negate everything He had spent hours telling His disciples two days earlier. No, Jesus never said anything like this.

To use John 14:2-3 and say that Jesus is telling His disciples "I am going to spare you tribulation and whisk you off to heaven, secretly", is a gross misinterpretation of scripture.

<u>Jesus had been teaching, as recorded in John chapters 13 through 17, that man can not go to heaven, but that His followers would enter into the "kingdom of heaven" also called the "kingdom of God". Both of these refer to an eternal existence with God. At the end of time, God is going to change his abode and live in the New Jerusalem. That is where you want to be, where God is.</u>

<u>Halley's Bible Handbook,</u> notes that the raising of Lazarus from the dead took place about a month before Jesus was crucified (544). In the chapter, "What Jesus Taught", it was discussed that Jesus had taught Martha, that His followers and sinners would be resurrected at the same time, at the "last day". So about a month before Christ died

on the cross, it is written in John that Christ had previously taught Martha that the resurrection of the just and unjust would be at the same time, at the "last day".

Then, two days before the Passover supper, or three days before His death, Christ told His disciples in great detail in Matt. 24 and 25, how the end of the world would come about, which includes judgments of the righteous and unrighteous at the same time.

Then we have the account in John 14, where Christ is telling His disciples, during the Passover, that He has to leave them, but that He will return for them. In the chapter of this book, "In My Father's House", it was explained that Jesus was telling them that He would return for them and they would spend eternity with Him in the new Jerusalem. They would enter into the new Jerusalem after the tribulation when Christ comes again.

In the three gospels, Matthew, Mark and Luke, Jesus taught He would return for His believers, "immediately after the tribulation of those days". Jesus tells His disciples that the sign to look for is <u>When the sun, moon and stars grow dark, then you know that Jesus Christ is about to return.</u>

Luke 21:25-28 And there shall be <u>signs in the sun, and in the moon, and in the stars</u>; and upon the earth distress of nations, with perplexity; the sea and the waves roaring; Men's hearts failing them for fear, and for looking after those things which are coming on the earth: for the powers of heaven shall be shaken. And then shall they see the <u>Son of man coming in a cloud with power and great glory</u>. And when these things begin to come to pass, then <u>look up, and lift up your heads; for your redemption draweth nigh</u>.

It Is Finished

9

Let's look at Daniel 9:27 and an explanation of the "abomination of desolation". The words in brackets [ ] are mine.

Daniel 9:27 (KJV) And <u>he</u> shall confirm the covenant with many for one week: [Jesus confirmed the existing covenant between God and man for seven years] *and in the midst of the week he shall cause the sacrifice and the oblation to cease,* [half way through the seven years He died on the cross and caused all sacrifices to end] *and for the overspreading of abominations he shall make it desolate,* [Christ, the ultimate sacrifice, made the temple sacrifices an abomination before God, hence the temple became desolate] *even until the consummation,* [when Christ comes again] *and that determined shall be poured upon the desolate* [Christ will judge the unbelieving desolate people].

You have probably heard that the Antichrist, when he arrives on the world scene, will make a seven-year peace treaty with Israel and then after 3½ years, break the treaty. This interpretation of Daniel 9:27 is widely accepted, but as you will see, has no Biblical basis. Prophecy teachers speak of it often as though it were true, sometimes without offering any Biblical proof. It has become widely accepted. Those that do, back up their claim using only the verse Daniel 9:27 shown above.

An in-depth study of Daniel chapter 9 will reveal that a prophecy speaking of the Messiah coming and making atonement for our sins has been twisted into a hypothetical scenario of the Antichrist making a peace treaty with the Jews. It is time to set the record straight and realize this whole passage of scripture is about Christ offering Himself as the ultimate sacrifice which ended animal sacrifices forever.

Proponents of this theory of a seven-year treaty use Daniel, chapter 9 to say that God's clock stopped counting the 490 years of this prophecy almost 2000 years ago when it had reached 483 years. They say the clock will start again after the rapture, because God owes the Jews seven more years of the total 490 years of the prophecy. They say the tribulation will take place during these last seven years, while the church is in heaven.

You will see, however, that God's clock never stopped. Jesus finished His mission concerning His first coming just as He said in John 19:30 and Luke 18:31. This will be discussed later in detail. Jesus does not owe the Jews anything more. His finished work on the Cross is all they will receive. All that remains is for them to believe. According to 1 John 2:23, anyone who does not believe on the Lord Jesus Christ as their personal savior is desolate and without God.

Turning back to Daniel chapter 9, the highly respected Bible commentator, Matthew Henry, says that the principal verses of this chapter, verses 24-27, refer to the Messiah, Jesus Christ. Henry makes no mention of the Antichrist making a treaty.

Dr. Adam Clarke (1760-1832), one of the leading Bible scholars of all time, is chiefly remembered for writing a commentary on the Bible which took him 40 years to complete. Few can come close to his knowledge of the Bible and the ancient languages of the Bible. In his commentary, Clarke's Commentary, Dr. Clarke agrees entirely with Matthew Henry that this prophecy foretells Christ and His plan of redemption for the Jews and all mankind.

Quoting from the Matthew Henry Concise Commentary *"We have, in verses Daniel 9:24-27, one of the most remarkable prophecies of Christ, of his coming and his salvation. It shows that the Jews are guilty of most obstinate unbelief, in expecting another Messiah, so long after the time expressly fixed for his coming. The seventy weeks mean a day for a year, or 490 years. About the end of this period a sacrifice would be offered, making full atonement for sin, and bringing in everlasting righteousness for the complete justification of every believer. Then the Jews, in the crucifixion of Jesus, would commit that crime by which the measure of their guilt would be filled up, and troubles would come upon their nation."*

Daniel 9:27 is the only verse in the Bible that is used to say the Antichrist will make a seven-year peace treaty with the Jews and then break it after 3 ½ years.

Matthew Henry makes no mention of the Antichrist in his commentary in reference to Daniel 9:27. Neither does Dr. Adam Clarke in his commentary. Both of these learned and highly respected Englishmen lived and wrote before the Plymouth Brethren came up with their pre-tribulation rapture theory in the mid 1800's.

Dan 9:24 (KJV) Seventy weeks are determined upon thy people and upon thy holy city, to finish the transgression, and to make an end of sins, and to make reconciliation for iniquity, and to bring in everlasting righteousness, and to seal up the vision and prophecy, and to anoint the most Holy 25 Know therefore and understand, that from the going forth of the commandment to restore and to build Jerusalem unto <u>the Messiah</u> the Prince shall be seven weeks, and threescore and two weeks: the street shall be built again, and the wall, even in troublous times. 26 And after threescore and two weeks shall Messiah be cut off, but not for himself: and the people of the prince that shall come shall destroy the city and the sanctuary; and the end thereof shall be with a flood, and unto the end of the war desolations are determined. 27 And <u>he</u> shall confirm the covenant with many for one week: and in the midst of the week he shall cause the sacrifice and the oblation to cease, and for the overspreading of abominations he shall make it desolate, even until the consummation, and that determined shall be poured upon the desolate.

The "seventy weeks" is generally agreed to mean seventy weeks of years or 490 years according to Halley (349).

The big question concerns the phrase "he shall confirm the covenant" of verse 27. Does the "he" refer back to the Messiah in verse 25 or does the "he" refer to the prince in verse 26? The answer is the Messiah. This whole prophecy refers to Jesus, His ministry and His sacrifice on the cross "to make reconciliation for iniquity".

Verse 27 has absolutely nothing to do with the Antichrist making a treaty and then breaking it. If the "he" refers back to "the prince", then it would refer to Titus, the

Roman conqueror, who destroyed the temple in Jerusalem in 70 A.D. Those who say "the prince" represents the Antichrist, who will come out of a revived Roman empire say it is the same as the little horn of Daniel 7:25.

However, Daniel received the prophecy recorded in Daniel chapter 7 in the year 555 B.C. while he received the prophecy in chapter 9 about 15 years later in 539 B.C. These dates come from the commentary written by Dr. Adam Clarke (1760-1832), one of the leading Bible scholars of all time (vol. IV, 590,600). There is nothing in chapter 9 that even hints that it is a continuation of the vision Daniel had 15 years earlier recorded in chapter 7. There is no mention of a covenant in Daniel chapter 7.

The "he" in verse 27 refers to the "Messiah" of verse 26. In verse 27, "confirm the covenant" means to strengthen an existing covenant, not to create a new one. To "confirm the covenant" refers to:

(Dan 9:4 KJV) And I prayed unto the LORD my God, and made my confession, and said, O Lord, the great and dreadful God, keeping the covenant and mercy to them that love him, and to them that keep his commandments;

This is the only other time 'covenant' is used in Daniel chapter 9. Nothing suggests creating a covenant or treaty.

In The Open Bible, we find in the footnotes of Daniel chapter 9 the following: "The entire vision (verses 24-27) refers to the Messiah and his purpose to bring an end to sin" (1112).

Didn't Jesus' dying on the cross and his resurrection "bring in everlasting righteousness" (Dan 9:24) to those who would believe and confirm or strengthen the existing (Dan 9:4) or everlasting (Heb 13:20) covenant of God?

The word covenant is used six times in all of Daniel, twice in chapter 9, just as you have seen, and four times in chapter 11, verses: 22, 28, 30 and 32. Most Bible scholars acknowledge that Daniel chapter 11, verses 1-35 have already been fulfilled by Antiochus Epiphanes when he sacrificed pigs on the altar of the temple in 168 B.C.

Daniel 11:36- 12:10 describes the time of the end and the reign of the Antichrist. It should be noted that all verses containing the word "covenant" in all of Daniel have been fulfilled. Daniel 11:41-45 does not talk about a covenant, but describes the Antichrist invading the land of Israel. There is nothing in those verses about a treaty with the Jews or a rebuilt temple. Daniel chapter 7 also says nothing about a treaty and a rebuilt temple. It talks about the little horn (Antichrist) opposing God and persecuting His people for 3.5 years.

Halley's Bible Handbook, attributes the whole prophecy of Daniel chapter 9 to Christ. Halley says it gives the exact time of the ministry of Christ and His death in "the midst of the week" of verse 27 (349). This prophecy was attributed to Christ by most scholars until 1909, when C.I. Scofield published his version of the King James Bible and in his comments changed the 'he' of Daniel 9:27 and said it is the Antichrist.

Scofield said in the Introduction to his first edition published in 1909, "... that all of the many excellent and useful editions of the <u>Word of God left much to be desired</u>". It appears that Scofield set about to tell us all how to interpret the Word of God. Are his explanations inspired by God?

In his explanations to the Word of God, it appears that Scofield may have borrowed the words of Dr. Samuel Tregelles (1813-1875) when Scofield came up with the famous notion of the Antichrist instigating a seven-year peace treaty with Israel. The words in Scofield's notes are very similar to the writings of Tregelles as reported by the <u>Jamieson Fausset Brown Commentary</u> (757).

Quoting from the 1917 edition of the <u>Scofield Bible</u>, Scofield says: "The 'he' of verse 27 is the 'prince that shall come' of verse 26, whose people (Rome) destroyed the temple, AD 70. He is the same with the 'little horn' of chapter 7. He will covenant with the Jews to restore their temple sacrifices for one week (seven years), but in the middle of that time he will break the covenant and fulfill Dan. 12:11" (914-5).

It has already been demonstrated that the 'he' of verse 27 is not the same 'little horn' of chapter 7 (Antichrist) as Scofield said above. The "he" of verse 27 is the Messiah of verse 26.

The one week of (Dan 9:27) *And <u>he</u> shall confirm the covenant with many for one week:* began **when Jesus was baptized (Matt 3:13-17) in 25 A.D. and started his ministry. The middle of the** week was when he caused the sacrifices to cease: *and in the midst of the week he shall cause the sacrifice and the oblation to cease,...* This happened when Jesus died on the cross, April 3, 29 A.D., according to Adam Clarke in his commentary. (266 vol.V5). This date will be discussed in detail later in this chapter.

Matthew 27:51(KJV) " And, behold, the veil of the temple was rent in twain from the top to the bottom; and the earth did quake, and the rocks rent;".

When the veil (curtain) of the temple was torn in two, sacrifices were no longer acceptable to God. Jesus was the sacrifice to end all sacrifices forever. Although the Jews continued to offer their sacrifices in the temple, they were unacceptable to GOD. The week, the last seven years of the 490 year probationary period for the Jews, ended when the Jews had finally and totally rejected Jesus as evidenced by the trial and stoning of Stephen (Acts 6:8- Acts 7:60) in 32 A.D. Clarke confirms Stephen died in the year 32 A.D. (738 vol. V). Then the Gospel was taken to the Gentiles with (Saul's (Paul)) conversion (Acts 9) and Peter's visions (Acts 10).

C. I. Scofield said, in the 1917 edition of the <u>Scofield Reference Bible</u>, regarding the trial and stoning of Stephen, "It was the final trial of the nation" (the Jews) (1158).

Scofield also said "The Jews having rejected Stephen's witness to, and of them, the Gospel now begins to go out to 'all nations'" (1159).

Scofield must not have realized it but he made a profound statement that totally discredited everything he had previously said about the Antichrist making a seven year peace treaty.

Scofield said that the stoning of Stephen marked the end of the 490 year probation period for the Jews.

<u>*To mark the beginning and the ending of the last week, the last seven years of Daniel's prophecy, GOD intervened in both of these events in a similar manner*</u>*. The heavens were opened and Jesus saw the Spirit of God, and likewise, the heavens opened for Stephen and he saw Jesus at the right hand of God.*

(Matthew 3:16) And Jesus, when he was baptized,

went up straightway out of the water: and, lo, the heavens were opened unto him, and he saw the Spirit of God descending like a dove, and lighting upon him. (Acts 7:56) And said, Behold, I [Stephen] see the heavens opened, and the Son of man standing on the right hand of God.

Jesus died on the cross 3½ years after he started his ministry. The last 3½ years of the last week (7 years) of Daniel's 490 year prophecy was left to see if the Jews would accept Jesus as 'Messiah'. Jesus warned the Jews in Matthew 21:42-44 that the kingdom of God would be taken from them and given to a nation that would bear fruit. As stated above, the Jews again rejected the Gospel evidenced by the stoning of Stephen. The Jews were supposed "to anoint the most Holy" (Jesus) Dan 9:24, but instead they nailed him to the Cross.

As you will see later, a remnant did anoint Jesus as their King so that the prophecies of Daniel, Isaiah and Zechariah were fulfilled. However, the majority of the Jews continued in disbelief. When the GOSPEL went to the Gentiles that marked the END of the 70 weeks.

The last week or seven years of Daniel 9:27 began when Christ was baptized in 25 A.D. and ended in 32 A.D. when Stephen was stoned. Daniel's prophecy of seventy weeks was completed in the year 32 A.D. It should not be used to interpret end-time events.

The desolations in Daniel 9:27, refer to the desolations of the Jewish people. Anyone without Christ is desolate.

When Christ was before Pilate, the people, the Jews, wanted Jesus crucified and took full responsibility for His death. (Mat 27:25 KJV) ***Then answered all the people, and said, His blood be on us, and on our children.***

These words of Jesus were spoken about the Jews, just three days before He was to die. ***"Behold, your house is left unto you desolate"*** (Mat 23:38).

C.I. Scofield said, on page 915 of his 1917 edition of the Scofield Bible, that "he (Antichrist) will covenant with the Jews to restore their temple sacrifices for one week (seven years), but in the middle of that time he will break the covenant and fulfill Dan. 12:11".

(Dan 12:11 KJV) *And from the time that the daily sacrifice shall be taken away, and the abomination that maketh desolate set up, there shall be a thousand two hundred and ninety days.*

Scofield is saying that the Antichrist will disallow sacrifices after 3.5 years of the seven years and the abomination that makes desolate would be setup 1290 days later.

This means that the abomination would be set up 30 days after the Second Coming of Christ in judgment. There are 360 days in the Jewish calendar and 2,520 days in the entire seven year period. The middle is 1260 days plus 1,290 is 2,550 days or 30 days after the seven years has ended.

Daniel 12:11 has nothing to do with the Antichrist making a treaty with Israel. It foretells the abomination of the Jewish nation being setup 1,290 days <u>after Jesus died on the cross</u>.

Jesus is the "he" of Dan 9:27, which is reported by <u>Jamieson Fausset Brown Commentary</u> (756). "The abomination that maketh desolate" was setup 1290 days after Jesus died on the cross which ended the daily sacrifices. After Jesus died on the cross, which was the ultimate sacrifice, the Jews still offered sacrifices, but they were no longer acceptable to God. The 1290 days after "the sacrifices ended", marked the time when the Jews rejected Christ totally as evidenced when they stoned Stephen. Then the Gospel was taken to the Gentiles 1290 days after Christ died on the cross. This setup the "abomination of desolation" of the Jewish nation. This verse makes perfect sense when it is properly applied to Jesus Christ offering himself as the "ultimate" sacrifice to end all sacrifices.

Daniel 9:27 is the only reference to a seven-year time period and you now know that it refers to Jesus and not the Antichrist. You also know that the last week or seven-year period ended approximately 1977 years ago in the year 32 A.D.

Some Prophecy writers arrive at false conclusions by trying to fit certain events into a seven-year time frame, brought on by not understanding that this prophecy of Daniel was fulfilled shortly after Christ died and has absolutely nothing to do with trying to interpret end-time scripture. Others say that God's clock stopped and He owes the Jews seven more years. Where do they find this in the Bible? God is not giving the Jews a third chance. Christ was their first chance and Stephen was their second chance. No, they are in desolation and the abomination was setup when they rejected Christ the second time by stoning Stephen.

The claim that the Antichrist will make a treaty with Israel for seven years and then break it after 3 ½ years fails the test. Daniel chapter nine is the only reference used to make that claim, but that chapter speaks only of Christ and His sacrifice on the cross.

Some prophecy writers say that not all six parts of the prophecy outlined by Gabriel in Daniel 9:24 have been fulfilled. Some even say that Christ was not anointed during His first coming and the prophecy which reads *"and to anoint the most Holy "* will be fulfilled during the millennial reign of Christ. When Christ comes again, He will not need to be anointed. The whole world will know that He is the one and only true GOD. He will return as: KING OF KINGS AND LORD OF LORDS. (Revelation 19:16)

Jesus fulfilled the whole of the Daniel Chapter 9 prophecy almost two thousand years ago. Jesus was anointed by the people in Jerusalem as recorded in:

Matthew 21:1 (KJV) And when they drew nigh unto Jerusalem, and were come to Bethphage, unto the mount of Olives, then sent Jesus two disciples, 2 Saying unto them, Go into the village over against you, and straightway ye shall find an ass tied, and a colt with her: loose them, and bring them unto me. 3 And if any man say ought unto you, ye shall say, The Lord hath need of them; and straightway he will send them. 4 All this was done, that it might be <u>fulfilled which was spoken by the prophet</u>, saying, 5 Tell ye the daughter of Sion, Behold, thy King cometh unto thee, meek, and sitting upon an ass, and a colt the foal of an ass. 6 And the disciples went, and did as Jesus commanded them, 7 And brought the ass, and the colt, and put on them their clothes, and they set him thereon. 8 And a very great multitude spread their garments in the way; others cut down branches from the trees, and strowed them in the way. 9 And the multitudes that went before, and that followed, cried, saying, Hosanna to the son of David: Blessed is he that cometh in the name of the Lord; Hosanna in the highest.

Verse 4 above refers to the messages of these prophets:

Isaiah 62:11 Behold, the LORD hath proclaimed unto the end of the world, Say ye to the daughter of Zion, Behold, thy salvation cometh; behold, his reward is with him, and his work before him.

Zechariah 9:9 Rejoice greatly, O daughter of Zion; shout, O daughter of Jerusalem: behold, thy King cometh unto thee: he is just, and having salvation; lowly, and riding upon an ass, and upon a colt the foal of an ass.

Also Jesus was anointed by God as recorded in:

*Luke 4:16 (KJV) And he [Jesus] came to Nazareth, where he had been brought up: and, as his custom was, he went into the synagogue on the sabbath day, and stood up for to read. 17 And there was delivered unto him the book of the prophet Esaias.[Isaiah]. And when he had opened the book, he found the place where it was written, 18 The Spirit of the Lord is upon me, because he hath **anointed me** to preach the gospel to the poor; he hath sent me to heal the brokenhearted, to preach deliverance to the captives, and recovering of sight to the blind, to set at liberty them that are bruised, 19 To preach the acceptable year of the Lord. 20 And he closed the book, and he gave it again to the minister, and sat down. And the eyes of all them that were in the synagogue were fastened on him. 21 And he began to say unto them, This day is this **scripture fulfilled** in your ears.*

As further proof that Jesus fulfilled the Daniel prophecy of chapter 9, we have in His Words:

John 19:30(KJV) When Jesus therefore had received the vinegar, he said, It is finished: and he bowed his head, and gave up the ghost.

Arthur Pink, in his book, <u>Exposition of the Gospel of John</u>, concerning Christ's words, "It is finished" as He was dying on the cross wrote: "All things had been done which the law of God required; all things established which prophecy predicted; ... all things performed which were needed for our redemption. Nothing was left wanting" (245).

Jesus had confirmed this with the disciples just a few days earlier as recorded in *Luke 18:31 (KJV) Then he took unto him the twelve, and said unto them, Behold, we go up to Jerusalem, and all things that are written by the prophets concerning the Son of man shall be accomplished.*

An act of treason was committed by Scofield when he changed the total meaning of Daniel 9:27 and attributed to Satan, the work of the Holy Spirit. Scofield did this when he said the Antichrist will make a treaty, when for hundreds of years the great Bible scholars before Scofield taught that this verse meant the Messiah, Christ would strengthen the existing covenant.

This act fits the definition of blasphemy (Matthew 12:31-32). Likewise, when you attribute this verse to the Antichrist, you attribute an act of the Holy Spirit to Satan. So be careful!

When Christ died on the cross He caused all animal sacrifices, from that point on, to be an abomination before God. From the time of His death until Titus destroyed the temple in 70 A.D. all sacrifices in the temple were abominable to God. The unbelieving Jews were desolate and without God. Finally, the Temple ceased to exist in 70 A.D. and the sacrifices stopped.

The greatest "Abomination of Desolation" of all time was setup when the Jews did not accept Christ as the long-awaited Messiah.

This meant they were desolate. The pre-tribulationists reference the words of Christ in Matthew 24:15 and say that this refers to the Antichrist in a rebuilt temple.

Matthew 24:15 (KJV) When ye therefore shall see the abomination of desolation, spoken of by Daniel the prophet, stand in the holy place, (whoso readeth, let him understand:)

No, Jesus was warning His disciples, gathered about Him, of the coming destruction of the Temple and of Jerusalem. This verse was fulfilled in 70 A.D. by Titus when he destroyed the Temple, just as Jesus had predicted in Matthew 24:2. It has nothing to do with the future Antichrist. The reason is found in the words "holy place".

If the temple in Jerusalem is rebuilt, it will not be a "holy place". God will not be there. At the time Jesus spoke the words, "holy place" (Matt. 24:15) in 29 A.D., the Temple in Jerusalem was still "Holy" before God. But after the crucifixion of Christ and the stoning of Stephen, the temple was no longer Holy. It was desolate. God had departed from it.

A REBUILT TEMPLE IN JERUSALEM WILL NOT BE HOLY. IT WILL BE AN ABOMINATION BEFORE GOD.

Dr. Adam Clarke (1760-1832), was one of the leading Bible

scholars of all time. Few can come close to his knowledge of the Bible and the ancient languages of the Bible. In Clarke's Commentary, he clearly attributes this warning of Christ given in Matthew 24:15 to the coming destruction of Jerusalem in 70 A.D. Dr. Clarke says that the followers of Christ heeded His warning and escaped Jerusalem and survived. He also said Josephus gives the number slain in all the sieges by the Romans at upwards of 1,357,660 and that 97,000 were taken captive (233, vol. 5).

Dr. Clarke wrote this commentary in 1798, about a hundred years before Mr. Scofield decided to change the generally accepted end-time beliefs and create his own summaries that contradicted the beliefs of great Bible scholars such as Dr. Adam Clarke.

Dr. Clarke puts the date of the crucifixion of Christ on April 3, 29 A.D. (266 vol. V).

The Jewish calendar has 360 days, so all calculations must be done based upon the 360 day year. We have 365.24 days in our year. This amounts to a difference of 7 X 5.24 or 36.68 days for the seven-year period.

Starting with the date of Christ's crucifixion April 3, 29 A.D. and going back 3½ years (1260 days) puts the date of Christ's Baptism in October of the year 25 A.D. Starting with the date of Christ's crucifixion April 3, 29 A.D. and going forward 3½ years (1260 days) puts the end of the last seven years of Daniel's prophecy marked by the stoning of Stephen in September of the year 32 A.D.

Luke 3:23 tells us Jesus was about 30 years of age when He began His public ministry, right after His baptism in the year 25 A.D. Subtracting 30 years from the year 25 A.D. places the birth of Christ in the year 5 B.C. Most scholars agree with the birth of Christ on or near 5 B.C.

As you have seen when you properly attribute the **"he" of Daniel 9:27 to Jesus, not to the Antichrist** as Scofield said, then it is easy to compute the end of the 490 years, which was computed before as about September 15 in the year 32 A.D. If you say that verse 27 refers to the Antichrist making a treaty with Israel, you can not use verse 27 in your calculations. Because we properly attribute verse 27 to the promised Messiah, Christ, we can use it in our calculations.

Daniel 9:26 says after 483 years Messiah would be cut off. The key is the word "after", it does not say exactly when He would be cutoff only after the 483 years. The next verse 27 tells us exactly, "in the midst of the week". So add 3 and a half years to the 483 and you have exactly when Christ died and ended the temple sacrifices, forever.

So, the exact date of the promised messiah being cutoff or "dying" was given as 483 + 3.5 = 486.5 years from the time the "commandment was given to restore and to build Jerusalem". So this prophecy tells us that Christ would die on the cross exactly 486.5 years after the decree to rebuild Jerusalem. The decree was issued by Artaxerxes in 458 B.C. as recorded in Ezra chapter seven. So 458 B.C. + 457 puts it at 1 B.C. which is the same as 1 A.D. There is no year labeled "zero". Subtracting 457 from 486.5 gives the year 29.5 A.D., the time when Christ died on the cross. This agrees with Adam Clarke who puts the date of the **crucifixion of Christ on April 3, 29 A.D.** (266 vol. V) as noted before. Scofield said, "The date of the crucifixion is not fixed." (914). The reason Scofield made this statement is because he can NOT use verse 27 in reference to Christ and His death on the cross as it should be.

Instead Scofield had made the blasphemous claim that verse 27 is attributed to Satan's Antichrist and his seven year peace treaty with the Jews.

This is a blasphemous statement because it takes from the work of the Holy Spirit on the Cross and is used in the work of Satan's Antichrist.

Note: the dates are all approximate and can be off by a year or so, but do validate putting an end of the last seven years of Daniel's prophecy sometime in the years 31-33 A.D.

<u>Daniel's prophecy also tells us the date of the crucifixion of Christ.</u>

We need to call two more witnesses to affirm that the 490 years of Daniel's prophecy ended sometime in the years 31-33A.D., just 3½ years after Jesus died on the cross.

First, as Jacob was about to die he told his sons what would happen to them in the days to come. To his son Judah, the father of the Jews, Jacob said: *The scepter will not depart from Judah, nor the ruler's staff from between his feet, until he to whom it belongs shall come and the obedience of the nations be his.* (Genesis 49:10 TNIV).

Jacob said that Judah had a high place as ruler, but when the real ruler, the Messiah, Christ would come Judah would relinquish authority.

The prophet Isaiah also spoke of Judah relinquishing authority: *"This is what the Lord, the LORD Almighty, says: "Go, say to this steward, to Shebna, who is in charge of the palace: ... "Beware, the LORD is about to take firm hold of you and hurl you away, ... I will depose you from your office, and you will be ousted from your position".*

"In that day I will summon my servant, <u>Eliakim</u> son of Hilkiah. ... I will place on his shoulder the key to the house of David; what he opens no one can shut, and what he shuts no one can open. I will drive him <u>like a peg into a firm place</u>; he will become a seat of honor for the house of his father. ... "In that day," declares the LORD Almighty, "the peg driven into the firm place will give way; it will be sheared off and will fall, and the load hanging on it will be cut down." The LORD has spoken. (Isaiah 22:15-25 TNIV).

The preceding is a prophecy telling how Shebna who represents Judah would fall from his secure place of authority and be replaced by Eliakim who represents Christ. Many rush to the quick but false conclusion that Eliakim is the one to fall, but this is not true. Reason for a moment, Isaiah has already told you that Shebna would be "ousted from your position". Eliakim has been described as *I will place on his shoulder the key to the house of David; what he opens no one can shut, and what he shuts no one can open.*

There is only one person that fits this description: Jesus Christ. The same words are repeated in Revelation describing Christ: *These are the words of him who is holy and true, who holds the key of David. What he opens no one can shut, and what he shuts no one can open. (Revelation 3:7 TNIV).*

No, Jesus has not fallen from His firm place. Judah has been replaced by Jesus Christ.

These two prophets have just told us that the promised Messiah, Christ would replace Judah.

The Jews (Judah) relinquished their power to Christ and now because of their rejection of Christ, are a desolate people. God doesn't owe them any more time. They are finished, unless they recognize Christ as the promised Messiah.

Halley's Bible Commentary records that Queen Victoria, Queen of England from 1836-1896, who was deeply touched by a sermon of F. W. Farrar on the Lord's Second Coming, said to him, "Dean Farrar, I should like to be living when Jesus comes, so that I could lay the crown of England at his feet" (447).

This shows that the Queen was a believer and that Dean Farrar taught the truth about the Second Coming. If he had been teaching a secret rapture, then she could not lay the crown at the feet of Christ. This same F. W. Farrar in his book, The Life and Work of St Paul, wrote "Four years after Jesus had died upon the cross of infamy, Stephen was stoned for being His disciple and His worshipper;" (555).

This is another confirmation of the 3.5 year interval between the death of Christ and the death of Stephen. With the Jews rejecting the message of Stephen telling them that they had just killed the promised Messiah, the 490 years ended for the Jews and the message then went to the Gentiles. Daniel's chapter 9 prophecy had been completely fulfilled.

Daniel's prophecy of seventy weeks or 490 years has been fulfilled. The last week or seven years of Daniel 9:27 began when Christ was baptized in 25 A.D. and started His ministry. God marked the beginning of the week: "And Jesus, when he was baptized, went up straightway out of the water: and, lo, the heavens were opened unto him, and he saw the Spirit of God descending like a dove, and lighting upon him" (Matthew 3:16).

The last week ended in 32 A.D. when Stephen was stoned. God marked the end of the week with the heavens opening just as He had marked the beginning. "And said, Behold, I [Stephen] see the heavens opened, and the Son of man standing on the right hand of God" (Acts 7:56).

Dan 9:27 (KJV) And he [JESUS] shall confirm the covenant with many for one week came true.

No Rebuilt Temple Needed

10

The pre-tributionists teach that there must be a rebuilt temple in Jerusalem to fulfill Bible prophecy. The following verses are used to say that the temple must be rebuilt.

2 Thessalonians 2:3-4 (KJV) Let no man deceive you by any means: for that day shall not come, except there come a falling away first, and that man of sin be revealed, the son of perdition; Who opposeth and exalteth himself above all that is called God, or that is worshipped; so that he as God sitteth in the temple of God, showing himself that he is God.

Revelation 11:1 (KJV) And there was given me a reed like unto a rod: and the angel stood, saying, Rise, and measure the temple of God, and the altar, and them that worship therein.

What is the "**temple of God**" in the New Testament? The Apostle Paul answered this question for us in his letters to the church at Corinth and to the church at Ephesus.

*1 Corinthians 3:16 (KJV) Know ye not that ye are the **temple of God**, and that the Spirit of God dwelleth in you? 17 If any man defile the temple of God, him shall God destroy; for the temple of God is holy, which temple ye are.*

*2 Corinthians 6:16 (KJV) And what agreement hath the temple of God with idols? for **ye are the temple of the living God**; as God hath said, I will dwell in them, and walk in them; and I will be their God, and they shall be my people.*

Ephesians 2:19-22 (KJV) Now therefore ye are no more strangers and foreigners, but fellowcitizens with the saints, and of the household of God; And are built upon the foundation of the apostles and prophets, Jesus Christ himself being the chief corner stone; In whom all the building fitly framed together groweth unto an holy temple in the Lord:

Adam Clarke, who wrote Clarke's Commentary, agrees that in 2 Thessalonians 2:4, Paul is speaking of the Antichrist being in a Christian Church, not a temple in Jerusalem. Clarke says: "so that sitting in the temple of God - having the highest place and authority in the Christian Church, he acts as God taking upon himself God's titles and attributes, and arrogating to himself the authority that belongs to the Most High".

Israelis in a rebuilt temple in Jerusalem are not the worshipers in Revelation chapter 11. The Antichrist will not waste his time on them. He knows they are his for all eternity unless they repent and accept Jesus Christ as their personal savior. No, Christians are the "temple of God" and the ones to be counted. Instead, the Antichrist will set himself up in a Christian Church and try to deceive those who believe and trust in Jesus Christ. These are the true worshipers of God, the New Testament **temple of God (1 Corinthians 3:16-17).**

The Abingdon Bible Commentary, in reference to Revelation 11:1 says, "Temple, altar and worshipers in John's interpretation stand for the Christian community of God". ... "the earthly Jerusalem is Sodom" (1384) in reference to Revelation 11:8.

Jesus told the Jews in *Matthew 23:37-39 (KJV) O Jerusalem, Jerusalem, thou that killest the prophets, and stonest them which are sent unto thee, how often would I have gathered thy children together, even as a hen gathereth her chickens under her wings, and ye would not! Behold, your house is left unto you desolate. For I say unto you, Ye shall not see me henceforth, till ye shall say, Blessed is he that cometh in the name of the Lord.*

Jesus told the Jews, *"your house is left unto you desolate"* and they would not see him until they proclaimed him the Messiah. Jews that deny Jesus do NOT have God the Father and are not worshipers of God. They rejected God when they rejected Jesus.

1 John 2:22-23 (KJV) Who is a liar but he that denieth that Jesus is the Christ? He is Antichrist, that denieth the Father and the Son. Whosoever denieth the Son, the same hath not the Father: (but) he that acknowledgeth the Son hath the Father also.

Therefore, anyone who denies that Jesus is the Christ (Messiah) does not have God the Father.

Jesus said in *John 10:30 (KJV) I and my Father are one.*

The Jews may get a temple built in Jerusalem but it will not be the one referenced in 2 Thessalonians 2 and Rev. 11 above. To even suggest such a thing is a horrible abomination unto God. Why did He have the last one destroyed?

<u>The Jews can Not WORSHIP GOD without FIRST acknowledging Jesus as the Messiah</u>. (1 John 2:23).

There is so much misplaced attention given to Israel today. You must realize Jesus is not there. It is a desolate place. Today, Israel is a nation of atheists because they reject Christ. Paul warned us to forget the present city of Jerusalem, but to look for the New Jerusalem that is above. It's too bad all the time and money spent taking Christians to Israel isn't better used winning the lost for Christ.

Galatians 4:22-26 (NIV) For it is written that Abraham had two sons, one by the slave woman and the other by the free woman. His son by the slave woman was born in the ordinary way; but his son by the free woman was born as the result of a promise These things may be taken figuratively, for the women represent two covenants. One covenant is from Mount Sinai and bears children who are to be slaves: This is Hagar. Now Hagar stands for Mount Sinai in Arabia and corresponds to the present city of Jerusalem, because she is in slavery with her children. But the Jerusalem that is above is free, and she is our mother.

The Jews may get a temple built in Jerusalem but it will not be the one referenced in 2 Thessalonians 2 and Revelation 11 above. You [Believers in Christ] are the Temple of God. To fulfill scripture, a temple in Jerusalem is NOT needed. Keep your eyes on JESUS not Jerusalem.

DECEPTION: When the Antichrist takes over a Christian Church, He will deceive many Christians who have been told the ANTICHRIST will set himself up as God in a rebuilt temple in Jerusalem.

None Saved During Tribulation

11

The eternal destiny of many millions of souls is at stake. The world's greatest revival, that some say will occur at the beginning of the tribulation, will never take place. The two witnesses of Revelation chapter 11 will be prophesying during the tribulation, however, there are No verses in the Bible of anyone repenting and receiving salvation. Countless millions of souls are at peril. This countless multitude whose eternal destiny is at stake is made up of two groups:

Those who will never hear the gospel or be witnessed to because Christians believe the greatest of revivals will take place after the Church has been raptured and is in heaven.

Those who attend the Church but have no real love for the truth, and will fall prey to the deception of the Antichrist as outlined in chapter one.

The Church needs to realize: ... *Satan himself is transformed into an angel of light. Therefore it is no great thing if his ministers also be transformed as the ministers of righteousness* .... *2 Corinthians 11:14-15*.

Misinterpreting the number 144,000 puts millions of souls at peril. The world's greatest revival, which some say will occur during the early part of the tribulation, will never happen. Millions will spend eternity with Satan because we are NOT doing everything we can NOW to reach the lost for Christ. Instead, we sleep while being fed the prosperity gospel, better described as: "what their itching ears want to hear" (2 Timothy 4:3).

In chapter one of the book of Revelation, Jesus appears to the apostle John and tells him to write about the things that he is about to see. In the seventh chapter of the book of Revelation, John speaks of a redeemed multitude, so great it could not be counted, that had endured the great tribulation, had washed their robes white and were standing before the throne of the Lamb. Very close scrutiny of this multitude is required.

If there will be a rapture of believers before the tribulation begins, then this multitude John is writing about **must receive salvation during the tribulation** because all those who were Christians before the tribulation began have already departed earth according to that theory.

Chapter seven of the book of Revelation very clearly states that a redeemed multitude had endured the tribulation. Why weren't they previously raptured? Pre-tribulationists claim that this multitude received salvation during the tribulation. It looks like the explanation came first, then verses were found to substantiate it. You will see that their choice of scripture, Revelation chapter 7, will not pass the test. The redeemed multitude were Christians before the tribulation began.

That is why winning lost souls now is so important, there won't be a second chance for them.

No one gets saved during the tribulation.

Chapter seven of the book of Revelation begins with John seeing four angels about to harm the earth. Then John sees a fifth angel who tells the other four angles not to hurt the land or the sea until he had placed a seal upon the foreheads of "the servants of our God".

Revelation 7:1 (NIV) After this I saw four angels standing at the four corners of the earth, holding back the four winds of the earth to prevent any wind from blowing on the land or on the sea or on any tree. 2 Then I saw another angel coming up from the east, having the seal of the living God. He called out in a loud voice to the four angels who had been given power to harm the land and the sea: 3 "Do not harm the land or the sea or the trees until we put a seal on the foreheads of the servants of our God."

Continuing with verse 4, John speaks of "hearing" the number of those who were sealed: 144,000 from all the tribes of Israel so they would be able to endure the wrath coming upon the earth. A point

NONE SAVED DURING TRIBULATION • 79

to remember is that John "heard", he did not "see" the number who were sealed.

Revelation 7:4-8 (NIV) Then I heard the number of those who were sealed: 144,000 from all the tribes of Israel. From the tribe of Judah 12,000 were sealed, from the tribe of Reuben 12,000, from the tribe of Gad 12,000, from the tribe of Asher 12,000, from the tribe of Naphtali 12,000, from the tribe of Manasseh 12,000, from the tribe of Simeon 12,000, from the tribe of Levi 12,000, from the tribe of Issachar 12,000, from the tribe of Zebulun 12,000, from the tribe of Joseph 12,000, from the tribe of Benjamin 12,000.

In Revelation 7:9-14 John tells of "seeing" a redeemed multitude, so great it could not be counted, that had endured the great tribulation, had washed their robes white and were standing before the throne of the Lamb.

Revelation 7:9 (NIV) After this I looked and there before me was a great multitude that no one could count, from every nation, tribe, people and language, standing before the throne and in front of the Lamb. They were wearing white robes and were holding palm branches in their hands.

Revelation 7:13-14 (NIV) Then one of the elders asked me, "These in white robes--who are they, and where did they come from?" I answered, "Sir, you know." And he said, "These are they who have come out of the great tribulation; they have washed their robes and made them white in the blood of the Lamb.

In verse 4, John "heard" the number that were sealed, 144,000 from all the tribes of Israel. What John heard was an angel describing the number that were being sealed.

The best way for the angel to do this was to use numerology that John could understand. The angel told John using numbers that represented a very large number or a complete number.

In verse 9, John "saw" the multitude so great it could not be counted. This is the same multitude described earlier as the 144,000 as you will see explained by many leading Bible authorities.

Many Bible expositors overlook the fact that John first **"heard"** the number that were sealed (Rev 7:4). The numbers John heard were given to him to convey a countless multitude. As you will see the numbers John heard were used to denote completeness. It is not a literal number. And then "After this I looked and there before me was **a great multitude**" (Rev 7:9). In the first case, John "heard" the number 144,000 that were to be sealed to endure the tribulation. Later, John saw the number that had been sealed as "**a great multitude that no one could count, from every nation, tribe, people and language**" that had come out of the tribulation and were before the throne of Christ.

The 144,000 and the redeemed multitude are the same group. There is no exit for Christians before the tribulation. The 144,000 were Christians before the tribulation began.

Many leading Bible authorities agree that the 144,000 and the redeemed multitude are one and the same. They are Christians of every race and color who are sealed to endure the tribulation which John "heard" being described as the 144,000. And later, after the tribulation, John "saw" the same group as the great multitude before the throne of Christ. They had endured the tribulation and had washed their robes white in the blood of the Lamb.

Dr. Henry H. Halley said it is a symbolical number. He wrote in his <u>Halley's Bible Handbook 1965</u>: "144,000 is the square of 12, multiplied a thousandfold, and is thought to be understood, **not numerically, but symbolically**, representing the Sum Total of the Elect of Israel ... or the Sum Total of Christians" (714).

If we say that the 144,000 is an exact literal number and do not believe what Dr. Halley and other leading authorities wrote, as will be shown, then we follow the group that says it is an exact literal number. If it is taken to be a literal number, then it will be demonstrated that exactly 144,000 people will spend eternity with Christ, no more. This is the same problem that the Jehovah's Witnesses had with their 144,000 in heaven which caused them to have to amend their teachings.

In the chapter of this book, "It is Finished" it was explained how the pronoun "he" has erroneously been applied, by some writers, to the wrong subject in the preceding verse (Daniel 9:26-27). By doing so, false conclusions such as the Antichrist making a seven-year peace treaty with Israel and the notion of the tribulation spanning seven years have been perpetrated upon an unsuspecting body of believers.

NONE SAVED DURING TRIBULATION ▪ 81

Likewise, the eternal destiny of millions of souls depends on how the number 144,000 found in Revelation 7:4 (NIV) is interpreted. "Then I heard the number of those who were sealed: 144,000 from all the tribes of Israel."

Is this a literal 144,000 or is it a symbolic number representing a vast multitude as many leading authorities believe?

From 1941 to 1959, Dr. Ray Summers taught a course in the interpretation of Revelation at Southwestern Baptist Theological Seminary in Fort Worth, Texas. From 1959 to 1964, he was professor of New Testament interpretation at Southern Baptist Theological Seminary in Louisville. In the fall of 1964 he moved to Baylor University, where he was Chairman of the Religion Department. In his book, <u>Worthy Is The Lamb</u>, in reference to the identity of the 144,000 of Revelation chapter seven, Summers writes:

"The 144,000 of the first consolatory vision represent not Jewish Christians only but the whole body of believers. ... 144,000 is used to represent absolute completeness; not one member of the true body of believers is lost" (150).

In reference to the visions of the 144,000 and the great multitude of Rev 7:9, Summers writes: "The two visions must represent the same group under different circumstances" (150).

According to the <u>Holman Bible Handbook 1992</u>, "Clearly John was referring to Christians as the 144,000 ... the 144,000 comprise the full number of God's people ... " (797). "In the second vision (7:9-17) the 144,000 have become 'a great multitude, which no one could count.'" (798).

<u>The Interpreter's Bible 1957</u> states "... he [John] has allegorized the twelve tribes to signify the Christians, composed of every people and nation ... who are the true Israel ... " (419).

According to the preceding sources, the great multitude in Rev 7:9-14, are Christians who have been sealed by God (Rev 7:3-8) to endure the tribulation. The redeemed multitude of Revelation 7:9-17 are the same 144,000 that have been sealed by God as His own who will endure the tribulation. Some will become martyrs, but they will all come before the throne of the Lamb as the redeemed countless multitude.

According to Abingdon Bible Commentary 1929, "Those who were thus protected were the spiritual Israel, and John uses a traditional Jewish apocalyptic number, 144,000, to signify the completeness of Israel (v.4). ... The great host of v. 9 is the same as the 144,000 of v. 4."(1381).

New American Bible in its footnotes states, " *One hundred forty-four thousand:* the square of twelve (the number of Israel's tribes) multiplied by a thousand, symbolic of the New Israel ... that embraces people *from every nation, race, people and tongue (9)*" (394).

It should be apparent from the above mentioned sources, that the redeemed multitude of Rev 7:9 were Christians, servants of God, before the tribulation began. They were sealed (v. 4) to endure the trouble ahead.

For the pre-tribulation rapture theory to stand, this countless multitude of Revelation 7:9 MUST somehow receive salvation AFTER the tribulation has begun. They must Not have been Christians before the tribulation begins, because according to that theory, immediately after the rapture there will NOT be one Christian alive on the earth. They will all have been taken off to heaven.

Revelation chapter seven does not support salvation for this multitude, which is made up of believers in Christ alive when the tribulation began. No one gets saved during the tribulation.

In addition, the eternal destiny of millions also is in question. Many Christians have been led to believe that, after they have been raptured, the world's greatest revival will soon take place with the real evangelists doing their work of winning souls, while they are enjoying being in heaven. If only this were true. This writer will always remember looking into the faces of skeptics in London's Hyde Park while preaching there many times standing on a ladder. To the great majority of the English, the Bible is a book of fairy tales. However, we can only believe what God's Word says, and it does not support a vast multitude receiving salvation after the tribulation begins.

The book, Revelation Unveiled, by Tim LaHaye, has on the back cover the caption "THE BIBLICAL FOUNDATION FOR

NONE SAVED DURING TRIBULATION ▪ 83

THE BEST-SELLING LEFT BEHIND SERIES". In this book, LaHaye declares, "Prior to the Tribulation, the Church will have been raptured. The 144,000 Israelite witnesses from all over the world will be converted ... These witnesses will harvest a multitude that no one can number (Rev. 7:9)" (235).

Let's look and see if the text of Revelation agrees with LaHaye. Assertion number one, that the Church will be raptured before the tribulation, was found to have no Biblical basis in previous chapters of this book. Many contradictions to that statement were outlined in the previous chapters.

Looking at assertion number two that 144,000 receive salvation can not be found in the above text of Revelation chapter seven. **Repentance precedes Salvation.** Where is repentance in all of the book of Revelation? Tell me if you can find it, Please!

Looking at assertion number three, that a vast multitude will receive salvation, also can not be substantiated for the same reasons as number two.

Revelation 9:20-21 (KJV) And the rest of the men which were not killed by these plagues yet **repented not** of the works of their hands, that they should not worship devils, and idols of gold, and silver, and brass, and stone, and of wood: which neither can see, nor hear, nor walk: **Neither repented they** of their murders, nor of their sorceries, nor of their fornication, nor of their thefts.

Revelation 16:9-11 (KJV) And men were scorched with great heat, and blasphemed the name of God, which hath power over these plagues: and they **repented not** to give him glory. And the fifth angel poured out his vial upon the seat of the beast; and his kingdom was full of darkness; and they gnawed their tongues for pain, And blasphemed the God of heaven because of their pains and their sores, and **repented not** of their deeds.

There is not a single verse that even suggests that anyone is saved during the tribulation. As you have seen in the scripture above, **the opposite is true. They all repented not.** Therefore, without repentance no one can receive salvation.

Jesus said: *I tell you, Nay: but, except ye repent, ye shall all likewise perish. Luke 13:3*

The Apostle Peter confirmed that repentance must precede salvation.

Acts 2:38 Then Peter said unto them, Repent, and be baptized every one of you in the name of Jesus Christ for the remission of sins, and ye shall receive the gift of the Holy Ghost.

There are NO verses in all of the book of Revelation indicating that anyone ever repented of their sins and received salvation.

One of today's best-selling study Bibles is the Life Application Bible. In their comments regarding the 144,000, it states: "The number 144,000 is 12 x 12 x 1,000, symbolizing completeness - **all** God's followers will be brought safely to him ..." (2312).

The Life Application Bible agrees that the two groups, the 144,000 and the redeemed multitude of Revelation 7:9, are the same with their comments on Revelation chapter seven:

"In verses 1-8 we see the believers receiving a seal to protect them through a time of great tribulation ...; in verses 9-17 we see the believers finally with God in heaven" (2313).

The claim LaHaye makes, cited above, that 144,000 "will be converted" and "will harvest a multitude that no one can number" is not supported by the Life Application Bible.

The second angel of Revelation 14:6-7 is proclaiming that the gospel of Jesus Christ is true. Summers writes, "It is the 'good tidings' or 'eternal gospel' of God's victory, and is followed by a call to all men to 'fear God, and give him glory'" (181).

It does not suggest anyone repents and receives salvation. At that time, it is too late to add any more names to the book of life (Rev. 20:15).

Since no one repents, no one is saved during the tribulation. John referred to the 144,000 as "the servants of our God". John defines "servants of our God" at the beginning of the book of Revelation as one who serves the Living God, such as himself.

Revelation 1:1 (NIV) The Revelation of Jesus Christ, which God gave unto him, to show unto his servants things which must shortly come to pass; and he sent and signified it by his angel unto his servant John:

NONE SAVED DURING TRIBULATION • 85

The servants are the Christians in the seven churches that Christ addresses personally telling them of their strengths and weaknesses in the first three chapters of Revelation. If the theory of the pre-tribulation rapture is true, wouldn't these 144,000 "servants of God" have been taken off to heaven?

In the book of Romans, Paul tells us that the old order of bloodlines has been replaced by faith in Christ. The only blood that matters is the shed blood of Christ given for the remission of the sins of those who believe.

Romans 2:29 (KJV) But he is a Jew, which is one inwardly; and circumcision is that of the heart, in the spirit, and not in the letter; whose praise is not of men, but of God.

Therefore, the 144,000 consist of those who believe in the Lord Jesus Christ. Race has nothing to do with it. The Apostle Paul states it even clearer in Galatians:

Galatians 3:26 (KJV) For ye are all the children of God by faith in Christ Jesus. 28 There is neither Jew nor Greek, there is neither bond nor free, there is neither male nor female: for ye are all one in Christ Jesus. 29 And if ye be Christ's, then are ye Abraham's seed, and heirs according to the promise.

John, the author of Revelation, defines "Jew" for us. Jesus is telling the church in Smyrna that there are people there claiming to be His people, (Jews), but they are not. They belong to Satan's group.

Revelation 2:9 (KJV) I know thy works, and tribulation, and poverty, (but thou art rich) and I know the blasphemy of them which say they are Jews, and are not, but are the synagogue of Satan.

There are two groups of people, those who belong to God which he calls Jews and those that belong to Satan. No one, today, can prove they are physical descendants of Abraham, Isaac and Jacob through bloodlines. <u>The only blood that counts today is the shed blood of Jesus Christ</u>.

Jesus caused the Roman, Titus to destroy the temple at Jerusalem in 70 A.D. He also had all temple records destroyed to abolish the old order. All citizens of New Jerusalem will have God's name in their forehead. Revelation 22:3-4 describes the inhabitants of the New Jerusalem.

86 • SET UP TO WORSHIP THE ANTICHRIST

Revelation 22:3 (KJV) And there shall be no more curse: but the throne of God and of the Lamb shall be in it; and his servants shall serve him: 4 And they shall see his face; and his name shall be in their foreheads.

For citizenship in the New Jerusalem, you must have God's name in your forehead. If you are still alive and not part of the 144,000 that will get sealed in Revelation 7:1-8, then You do NOT have citizenship in the New Jerusalem. It is the only time God's servants get sealed in all of the book of Revelation.

The same 144,000 are pictured again in Revelation 14:1-5 as the redeemed multitude before the throne of God, after the tribulation. Here they are pictured with the Lamb (Christ) singing a song that only the 144,000 could sing.

<u>Once again the number 144,000 is a number of completeness, not a literal number.</u>

They are described as pure, because they had come out of the tribulation and had kept themselves spiritually pure. They had not worshiped the beast or taken his mark. Therefore, the 144,000 are according to Halley, the "Total of the Elect of Israel, the Firstfruits of the Gospel, or the Sum Total of Christians" (714).

We will say it again, **the 144,000 of Revelation 7:4 are the same as the "great multitude" of Revelation 7:9. There is only one sealing in all of the Book of Revelation. It is in Revelation 7:4-8 when the 144,000 are sealed. The same 144,000 are pictured again in Revelation 14:1-5 as the redeemed before the throne of God.**

If the 144,000 and the countless multitude are two different groups as the pre-tribulation rapture theory teaches and the 144,000 is an exact literal number in Rev. 7:4, then it is an exact literal number in Rev. 14:1-5 and there will only be 144,000 souls in the kingdom of God, before the throne of the Lamb. So you should see that 144,000 has to be a number representing completeness or a great numberless multitude.

Since the two groups discussed above are one and the same, there will NOT be 144,000 super evangelists witnessing to and leading a countless multitude to Christ in the beginning of the tribulation. After the sealing of the servants of God in Revelation 7:1-8, placing

God's name in their foreheads, there will be no more added to the "redeemed multitude". That's it, the "book of life" (Rev. 20:15) will be complete. No more names will ever be added to it.

There will NOT be 144,000 Jews that somehow get saved and become super evangelists and win countless millions to Christ during the early part of the tribulation. There is not one verse in all of the book of Revelation to support that claim. Repentance must precede Salvation. There is no repentance.

The words "repent" and/or "repented" are used only four times in all of the book of Revelation except for the warnings of Christ given to the churches to repent in the first three chapters of Revelation. In all of the remaining chapters we find only:

Revelation 9:20 (KJV) And the rest of the men which were not killed by these plagues yet repented not of the works of their hands, that they should not worship devils, and idols ...21 Neither repented they of their murders, nor of their sorceries, nor of their fornication, nor of their thefts. Revelation 16:9 (KJV) 9 And men were scorched with great heat, and blasphemed the name of God, which hath power over these plagues: and they repented not to give him glory.11 And blasphemed the God of heaven because of their pains and their sores, and repented not of their deeds.

A great multitude does not receive salvation during the tribulation. As you have seen above, **the opposite is true. They all repented not**. This sealing of Revelation chapter seven protects God's chosen from the locusts described here.

Revelation 9:3 (NIV) And out of the smoke locusts came down upon the earth and were given power like that of scorpions of the earth. 4 They were told not to harm the grass of the earth or any plant or tree, but <u>only those people who did not have the seal of God</u> on their foreheads. 5 They were not given power to kill them, but only to torture them for five months. And the agony they suffered was like that of the sting of a scorpion when it strikes a man. 6 During those days men will seek death, but will not find it; they will long to die, but death will elude them.

Another flaw in the theory of the escape or rapture before the tribulation is confirmed with the question: "How does the vast multitude of believers in Rev 7:9 get sealed, *if they are NOT the same group as the 144,000?" If these are two different groups, as that theory demands, then the multitude in Rev. 7:9 never does get sealed. Therefore, they will get tortured. Even more important: they will not have the seal of God, given only to the 144,000, and will not enter the New Jerusalem. (Rev. 22:3).*

Verse four above tells us that the locusts have power to hurt "only those people who do NOT have the seal of God on their foreheads".

If the vast multitude of Rev 7:9 receives salvation after God's servants (144,000) are sealed, then they will endure the torture of the locusts and will be excluded from the New Jerusalem. Could this theory of the escape before the tribulation be what God was talking about in Jeremiah?

Jeremiah 14:14 (NIV) Then the LORD said to me, "The prophets are prophesying lies in my name. I have not sent them or appointed them or spoken to them. They are prophesying to you false visions, divinations, idolatries and the delusions of their own minds."

How can you be sure that any theory is true and does not fit the description above in Jeremiah? The only way of course is to check it out with the Word of God, which is what has been done. We have found contradictions. If the countless multitude of Revelation 7:9 is Not the same group as the 144,000 that got sealed in Revelation 7:4-8, then they do Not have God's name written in their foreheads (Rev 22:4) and can NOT enter into the New Jerusalem with Jesus Christ. Remember there is only one sealing and it is described in Revelation 7:1-8.

The theory of the escape before the tribulation can not be substantiated by the Bible. Christians will be on earth to face the Antichrist. A countless multitude will NOT receive salvation during the tribulation.

Let's look at the fruit of this teaching. Christians are not witnessing to sinners about Christ because they think the real evangelists will do the work for them after they have been raptured. What about the millions who are dying each year without Christ? Are you going to stand before Christ and say, "Well, I didn't witness to anyone because they told me a great multitude would be saved during the tribulation". Jesus will answer: ***As long as it is day, we must do the work of him who*** *sent me. Night is coming, when no one can work (John 9:4).*

Millions of Christians are happy to hear about the great soul winning of the tribulation that will never take place, because they know they are not doing what Christ commanded them to do (Matthew 28). No verses can be found in Revelation to support anyone repenting and receiving salvation. It appears that once the tribulation starts, the door to salvation is closed.

We used to sing the song, "Onward Christian Soldiers" marching off to war. But these pre-tribulationists have declared that the Christian soldier will never see battle. He is going home before the real battle even begins. Don't you think Satan is delighted with their plan? Remember, he knows the Bible better than any of us (Matthew 4). Satan knows the countless multitude, which the pre-tribulationists say will be saved during the tribulation, will spend ALL eternity with him unless we wake up now and fight the battle for the souls of that countless multitude. Could Satan have planted the seeds of that theory? We are only doing what Paul commands us in 1 Thessalonians 5:21: *Test everything, Hold on to the good (NIV).*

The redeemed multitude, who had endured the tribulation and were before the throne of God (Rev. 7:9-14), are the same group as those 144,000 sealed by God (Rev 7:3-8) to endure the tribulation. This means:

- Christians will NOT exit earth before the tribulation begins
- A great multitude will NOT be saved during the tribulation.

Conflicting Conclusions

12

No one has advanced the theory of the rapture to heaven before the tribulation more than these two men: C.I. Scofield (Aug. 19, 1843 - July 24, 1921) and Tim LaHaye (April 27, 1926 -), the author of the "Left Behind" series of books.

Scofield, in his Scofield Reference Bible, was, possibly, one of the first to place his explanations of Scripture on the same page as the Holy Word. Scofield's views have been widely accepted as "Gospel" by many students of the Bible eager to know what God has in store for us all. Millions have been reading Scofield's notes since 1909, when his first edition became available and have believed his interpretations as though they were divinely inspired. The problem is that you are relying on one man's insights into God's Word. What if he is wrong?

Scofield wrote in his explanations: "The great tribulation is the period of unexampled trouble ... Its duration is three and a half years, or the last half of the seventieth week of Daniel (Dan. 9. 24-27, note; Rev. 11. 2,3)" (1337).

Scofield goes on to say on the same page, "The great tribulation will be, however, a period of salvation" (1337).

With these comments, Scofield places a "period of salvation" in the last half of the tribulation, or the last 3.5 years of the seven-year period which he called "the great tribulation".

It should be pointed out that in the chapter of this book, "It Is Finished", it was demonstrated that the last seven-year period of Dan. 9:24-27 ended with the stoning of Stephen on or about the year 32 A.D. However, for our discussion here, it is necessary to continue on with the false assumption that the last seven years of Daniel's prophecy is still in the future. Remember, Daniel 9:27 is the only verse in all of the Bible used to make the false claim of a seven-year tribulation. It should be emphatically stated that the period determined for the tribulation is 3 and a half years or less. This is given in Daniel 12:7, Revelation 12:14, and Revelation 13:5.

There are no verses in the entire Bible that speak of a seven-year period of time for the tribulation.

LaHaye says "As a special climax to God's ministry of salvation, Revelation 7:9 indicates that during the first part of Tribulation the greatest soul harvest in all history will take place" (153).

Scofield says that this period of salvation takes place in the last 3.5 years of the seven years, while LaHaye says that it is in the "first part of Tribulation" (153). LaHaye's book was published in 1999 and Scofield's was published in 1909.

Why, in just ninety years, has the time of salvation shifted from the last half of the tribulation to the beginning? Is this theory of the great revival so difficult to extract from scripture that it can not withstand the test of time, that is, an interval of just ninety years?

Remember from the last chapter of this book, "None Saved During Tribulation" it was demonstrated that in all of the book of Revelation there is no mention of anyone repenting.

Without repentance, there is no salvation.

These millions of souls will never be won for Christ because these two men have led Christians to believe that as soon as they leave earth in the rapture, the real evangelists will start to work.

Consider this: In Scofield's notes he mentions that: "The great tribulation will be, however, a period of salvation" (1337). Could it be that, while Scofield was searching for scripture which could be adjusted to fit a rapture before the tribulation he came across Revelation 7:9-16 which speaks of a great multitude who had endured the tribulation and were before the throne of God when he realized he had a problem? Why weren't they raptured with the others? The only possible answer: they receive salvation after the rapture. It appears that, for Scofield, salvation for the great multitude was an explanation for his dilemma, while for LaHaye it has moved to the forefront of his teachings.

Millions of souls will never be won for Christ because Scofield and LaHaye have led Christians to believe, as soon as they leave earth in the rapture, the real evangelists will start to work.

New Testament Church Is Israel

13

The best approach to Biblical Truth is to start with a clean slate, assume nothing, and then read through the Bible several times. God will reveal His truths to you. Then you will have real Biblical Truth that you can backup with book, chapter and verse. Using this approach it becomes apparent that those who say certain prophecies concerning Israel are being fulfilled today arrive at this conclusion incorrectly because they do not understand that Biblical Israel includes far more people that just those referred to as Jews. The Jews makeup just one-twelfth of Israel. Bible prophecy can not be fulfilled until all twelve tribes are included. This study will show you the difference between Hebrew, Israel, and Jew. It will also introduce you to Ephraim, one of the sons of Joseph. The Old Testament prophets Isaiah, Ezekiel, Hosea and Amos wrote about Ephraim. Their prophecies can not be properly understood until you realize that Ephraim's descendants are waiting to be regathered by Christ. These descendants of Ephraim are not Jews, but they makeup the majority of Israel today.

Many proclaim the Jews are God's Chosen People and if you are not a Jew you are a member of a subordinate group called Gentiles. However, an indepth study of the Bible, in the manner described above, will reveal that there is much more to this story. Our study starts in the book of Genesis.

God told Abraham that he would bless those who blessed him and curse those who cursed him (Genesis 12:3).

God entered into a covenant with Abram, changed his name to Abraham, gave him a son named Isaac and said that his covenant would be with Isaac (Genesis 17).

Isaac's son Jacob gets his father's blessing (Genesis 27).

The blessings given to Abraham are passed on to Jacob (Genesis 28:14).

Jacob wrestles with God and is blessed and given the name Israel (Genesis 32:22-29).

Israel (Jacob) had 12 sons: Reuben, Simeon, Levi, Judah, Issachar, Zebulum, Joseph, Benjamin, Dan, Naphtali, Gad and Asher (Genesis 35:22-26).

Abraham ---> Isaac ---> Israel (Jacob) ---> 12 sons (12 tribes of Israel)

Because of jealousy, Joseph was sold into slavery by his brothers. Joseph was taken down to Egypt. Joseph had two sons while he was in Egypt. Joseph's sons, Ephraim and Manasseh, would be reckoned as sons of Joseph's father, Jacob also known as Israel (Genesis 48:5).

The descendants of Ephraim would become a multitude of nations (Genesis 48:19).

<u>All the blessings given by God to Abraham, Isaac and Jacob were passed from Jacob to his son Joseph and to his sons Ephraim and Manasseh.</u>

... because of your father's God, who helps you, because of the Almighty, who blesses you with blessings of the heavens above, blessings of the deep that lies below, blessings of the breast and womb.

Your father's blessings are greater than the <u>blessings of the ancient mountains, than the bounty of the age-old hills.</u> Let all these rest on the <u>head of Joseph</u>, on the brow *of the prince among his brothers (Genesis 49:25-26).*

<u>The Major Blessings of God with all the good things of the earth are passed on to Joseph.</u> These are all then passed on to Ephraim and Manasseh by Moses.

*Deuteronomy 33:13 About **Joseph** he said: "May the LORD bless his land with the precious dew from heaven above and with the deep waters that lie below; 14* ***with the best the sun brings forth and the finest the***

*moon can yield; 15 with the choicest gifts of the ancient mountains and the fruitfulness of the everlasting hills; 16 with the best gifts of the earth and its fullness and the favor of him who dwelt in the burning bush. Let all these rest on the head of Joseph, on the brow of the prince among his brothers. 17 In majesty he is like a firstborn bull; his horns are the horns of a wild ox. With them he will gore the nations, even those at the ends of the earth. Such are the ten thousands of **Ephraim**; such are the thousands of Manasseh."*

The major blessings bestowed upon Ephraim and Manasseh were pronounced first by Jacob before he died in Egypt. Later, it was confirmed by Moses just before the children of Israel were to enter the promised land.

The sons of Reuben the firstborn of Israel (he was the firstborn, but when he defiled his father's marriage bed, <u>his rights as firstborn were given to the sons of Joseph</u> son of Israel; so he could not be listed in the genealogical record in accordance with his birthright, and though Judah was the strongest of his brothers and a ruler came from him, <u>the rights of the firstborn belonged to Joseph</u>) (1 Chronicles 5:1-2 NIV).

The right as first born son of Jacob goes to Ephraim and Manasseh because Reuben had defiled his father's bed (Genesis 35:22).

*... for **I am a father to Israel, and Ephraim is my firstborn** (Jeremiah 31:9-10).*

To Judah (ancestor of Jews) Jacob said *The scepter will not depart from Judah, nor the ruler's staff from between his feet, until he comes to whom it belongs and the obedience of the nations is his* (Genesis 49:10 NIV).

The scepter was rightfully passed to Christ, the one *to whom it belongs* when He died on the cross for the sins of all mankind.

The only blessing given to Judah by Moses was that he would return to his people (Deuteronomy 33:7).

This was fulfilled when the Jews, returned from Babylon (Ezra 1-2).

These verses have shown that the major Blessings of God given to Abraham, Isaac and Jacob were passed on to the two sons of Joseph, Ephraim and Manasseh, not to Judah.

98 ▪ SET UP TO WORSHIP THE ANTICHRIST

Because of the sins of Solomon worshiping other gods, God divided Israel into 2 parts: the Southern Kingdom made up of Judah and Benjamin and the Northern Kingdom made up of the other 10 tribes. The Northern Kingdom was called Israel or Ephraim. The Southern Kingdom was called Judah (1 Kings 11).

God warned Israel that they would be scattered if they didn't obey his commandments (Deuteronomy 28:64). They disobeyed God and were scattered as recorded in 2 Kings 15:29 and 2 Kings 17:6-7. Nelson's New Illustrated Bible Dictionary states: "Already in 732 B.C. Tiglath-Pileser III had carried Reuben, Gad and the half-tribe of Manasseh captive to Mesopotamia when Damascus fell" (361).

Holman Bible Handbook affirms that: "According to Assyrian records 27,290 inhabitants of Samaria were deported. The Assyrians resettled Israelites in Northeastern (Halah) and Northwestern (Gozan) Mesopotamia and in Media, the eastern frontier of their empire (2 Kgs 17:10)" (264).

The Open Bible New Living Translation in a footnote declares that the king of Assyria: "Sargon II (722-705 B.C.) took the throne shortly before Samaria fell in 722 B.C. In an inscription Sargon claims credit for deporting 27,290 captives" (512).

This fulfilled Isaiah's prophecy of Assyria being the instrument of God's judgment against the Northern Kingdom (Isaiah 10:5-6).

Jacob went to Egypt with his family of 70 men, women and children. (Gen. 46:27). Moses left Egypt with 600,000 men plus women and children 430 years later (Exodus 12:40).

If this same growth rate was experienced by the 27,290 Israelites that were deported in 722 B.C. from Samaria as was with the Israelites in Egypt, then there would be many millions of Israelites living outside of Palestine in the year 27 A.D. when Jesus was talking about the lost sheep of the house of Israel.

There were 27,290 men taken from Samaria, whereas 70 men went to Egypt. This means there were 389 times as many men deported from Samaria as there were that went to Egypt.

Then 430 years later in the year 292 B.C., there would be 389 times 600,000 or 233,400,000 Israelite men living outside of Palestine not called Jew. This number is far too high. The U.S. Census Bureau estimates the world's population in the year 500 B.C. at 100 million. They also estimate the number to be between 170-400 million in the year 1 A.D. An exact number can not be calculated nor is needed.

What is important is that when Christ was on the earth, the lost sheep of the house of Israel numbered at least a million.

When Christ said that He came only for the lost sheep of the house of Israel, He was referring to the million(s) of Israelites living outside of Palestine at that time.

The descendants of the lost tribes of Israel today are probably numbered in the tens or hundreds of millions, whoever and wherever they are. They are also God's Chosen People. No attempt will be given to identify these descendants. Jesus will identify them when He returns. The only purpose here is to state that they exist somewhere in the world today. The promises given to Abraham, Isaac, Jacob (Israel) were passed on to Israel's twelve sons. The Northern Kingdom that was taken captivity was made up of the descendants of eight of the sons of Israel plus **Ephraim and Manasseh** making up the ten tribes of Israel.

History does not accurately record what happened to these people but let's see what the Bible has to say about them.

2 Kings 17:23 (NIV) ... So the people of Israel were taken from their homeland into exile in Assyria, and they are still there.

Zechariah 10:7-9 (NIV) The Ephraimites will become like mighty men, and their hearts will be glad as with wine. Their children will see it and be joyful; their hearts will rejoice in the LORD. I will signal for them and gather them in. Surely I will redeem them; they will be as numerous as before. Though I scatter them among the peoples, yet in distant lands they will remember me. They and their children will survive, and they will return.

Jeremiah 31:10 (NIV) Hear the word of the LORD, O ye nations, and declare it in the isles afar off, and say, He that scattered Israel will gather him, and keep him, as a shepherd doth his flock.

*Hosea 11:8-9 (NIV) How shall I give thee up, **Ephraim**? how shall I deliver thee, Israel? ... I will not execute the fierceness of mine anger, I will not return to destroy **Ephraim**: for I am God, and not man; the Holy One in the midst of thee: ... .*

*Romans 11:26 (NIV) And so **all Israel** will be saved, as it is written: "The deliverer will come from Zion; he will turn godlessness away from Jacob.*

Paul is speaking of people from all 12 tribes of Israel

when he says "all Israel will be saved". It is wrong to say all natural born Jews will be saved.

Verses that speak of the Gathering of the people make a distinction between Israel (Ephraim) and Judah (Jews).

*Isaiah 11:11 (NIV) In that day the Lord will reach out his hand a second time to reclaim the remnant that is left of his people from Assyria, from Lower Egypt, from Upper Egypt, from Cush, from Elam, from Babylonia, from Hamath and from the islands of the sea. 12 He will raise a banner for the nations and gather the **exiles of Israel**; he will assemble the scattered **people of Judah** from the four quarters of the earth. 13 Ephraim's jealousy will vanish, and Judah's enemies will be cut off; **Ephraim will not be jealous of Judah, nor Judah hostile toward Ephraim.***

*Jeremiah 30:3 (NIV) The days are coming,' declares the LORD, 'when I will bring **my people Israel and Judah** back from captivity and restore them to the land I gave their forefathers to possess,' says the LORD."*

*Ezekiel 37:15 (NIV) The word of the LORD came to me: 16 "Son of man, take a stick of wood and write on it, 'Belonging to **Judah and the Israelites associated with him.**' Then take another stick of wood, and write on it, '**Ephraim's stick, belonging to Joseph and all the house of Israel associated with him.**' 17 Join them together into one stick so that they will become one in your hand. 18 "When your countrymen ask you, 'Won't you tell us what you mean by this?' 19 say to them, 'This is what the Sovereign LORD says: **I am going to take the stick of Joseph--which is in Ephraim's hand--and of the Israelite tribes associated with him, and join it to Judah's stick, making them a single stick of wood,** and they will become one in my hand.' 20 Hold before their eyes the sticks you have written on 21 and say to them, 'This is what the Sovereign LORD says: **I will take the Israelites out of the nations where they have gone. I will gather them from all around and bring them back into their own land. 22 I will make them one nation in the land, on the mountains of Israel. There will be one king over all of them and they will never again be two nations or be divided into two kingdoms.** 23 They will no longer defile themselves with their idols and vile images or with any of their offenses, for I will save them from all their sinful backsliding, and I will cleanse them. They will be my people, and I will be their God. 24 "**My servant David will be king over them, and they will all have one shepherd. They will follow my laws and be careful to keep my decrees.** 27 My dwelling place will be with them; I will be their God, and they will* *be my people. 28 Then the nations will know that I the LORD make Israel holy, when my sanctuary is among them forever.'"*

Notice the distinction that Ezekiel made between Judah and Ephraim. These verses in Ezekiel are waiting to be fulfilled. The notion that the 10 tribes were destroyed completely is refuted by God: *I will not carry out my fierce anger,* **nor will I turn and devastate Ephraim***. For I am God, and not man-- the Holy One among you. I will not come in wrath. 10 They will follow the LORD; he will roar like a lion. When he roars, his children will come trembling from the west. (Hosea 11:9).*

The King James Version first uses the name **Jews** in 2 Kings 16:6 whereas the NIV says "the people of Judah". "Jews" was first used in the NIV in Ezra to reference those of Judah who had gone to rebuild the Temple in Jerusalem. This was approximately 450 B.C.

In 539 B.C., 183 years after the Northern Kingdom was taken into captivity in 722 B.C. , there were many of God's Chosen People (Israelites) living outside of Palestine. Daniel confirms this: *"Lord, you are righteous, but this day we are covered with shame—the people of Judah and Jerusalem and all Israel, both near and far, in* **all the countries where you have scattered us because of our unfaithfulness to you.** *(Daniel 9:7 TNIV).*

Abraham was not a Jew, neither was Isaac, nor Israel or 11 out of the 12 tribes. Only the tribe of Judah can properly be called Jew. Also the promises God made to Abraham in Genesis 12:3 apply to all the descendants of Abraham, Isaac, and Jacob (Israel). This includes those millions identified by Hosea.

Hosea 1:10 (NIV) Yet the number of the children of Israel shall be as the sand of the sea, which <u>cannot be measured nor numbered</u>; and it shall come to pass, that in the place where it was said unto them, ***Ye are not my people, there it shall be said unto them, Ye are the sons of the living God.*** *11 Then shall the children of* ***Judah and the children of Israel be gathered together, and appoint themselves one head****, and they shall come up out of the land: for great shall be the day of Jezreel.*

Hosea 8:8 (NIV) **Israel** *is swallowed up; now she is among the nations like a worthless thing.*

Hosea 9:13 (TNIV) I have seen **Ephraim***, like Tyre, planted in a pleasant place. But Ephraim will bring out their children to the slayer."*

Could the slayer be the abortionist?

The special blessings of God given only to Manasseh and Ephraim can not be taken away.

(Rom 11:29 NIV) for God's gifts and his call are irrevocable.

Therefore these gifts given by GOD to Manasseh and Ephraim and their multitude of descendants are irrevocable. This is a key point in Biblical research that has been overlooked by most writers. It is one of the reasons so many other parts of the Bible are misinterpreted. The name Manasseh is used 143 times in 132 verses in the King James Bible. The name Ephraim is used 172 times in 155 verses in the King James Bible.

When many people read their Bible and come across these two names they say it is talking about the Jews, but this is false. Manasseh and Ephraim were not Jews. They were born about 1970 B.C. in Egypt.

The first time anyone was called "Jew" is recorded in the King James Bible in 2 Kings 16:6. This was during the reign of King Ahaz of Judah in about 738 B.C. Here the New International Version (NIV) uses the phrase "men of Judah". In the NIV, the first time anyone was called "Jew" was 200-300 years later as recorded in Ezra 4:12. Jew was a name given to the people from the tribes of Judah and Benjamin who had been deported to Babylon in 586 B.C. and 70 years later allowed to return to Palestine.

The only people that can be rightfully called Jew are descendants from the tribe of Judah, one of the 12 sons of Israel. Ephraim and Manasseh are Israelites and part of "God's Chosen People" but are not Jews.

The 2 sons of Joseph, Ephraim and Manasseh were reckoned as sons of Israel. Ephraim and Manasseh received many special gifts that the other Israelites did not receive and they were reckoned as the firstborn of Israel because Reuben had defiled his father's marriage bed (Genesis 35:22),(1 Chronicles 5:1-2).

All the special rights of the first born son of Israel, the famous patriarch of modern day Jewry went to descendants of Israel that have never been called "Jew".

This is only a synopsis of a major topic to be covered in the next book <u>Israel Is Not Real Estate</u>. This demonstrates that unless one has a proper understanding of the difference between Israel and Jew, one can not properly understand Bible prophecy. Jew, Israelite and Hebrew are not the same. The King James Bible uses the words "Jew(s)" 270 times, whereas; it uses the word "Israel" 2566 times in 2294 verses. "Israel" is first used to make reference to Jacob, the patriarch. Then it is also used to make a reference to the ten tribes (all except Judah and Benjamin). Sometimes, "Ephraim" is used to denote the ten tribes as seen before in Hosea.

Understanding the people of Israel requires tracing their ancestry starting with Abraham before you can comprehend the difference between Hebrew, Israelite and Jew. They are not synonymous. For example, Abram who had his name changed to Abraham by God (Gen. 17:5) was not a Jew, instead he was Hebrew. *Gen 14:13 And there came one that had escaped, and told <u>Abram the Hebrew</u>.* Therefore, it is wrong to call Abraham a Jew. Abraham lived about 1,500 years before anyone was called a "Jew".

To really understand Bible prophecy you must first study God's special people, the Israelites. Most Israelites are NOT Jewish.

This has been a brief outline of the blessings given by God to those born the natural way into His chosen people, the Israelites. However, those who are born-again believers in Jesus Christ have citizenship in the Spiritual Israel, the one that lasts for eternity. The real difference is those born the natural way into His chosen people have blessings good only for this lifetime. Those born-again into Spiritual Israel have blessings good for all eternity.

As Paul says in *Ephesians 2:10 For we are God's workmanship, created in Christ Jesus to do good works, which God prepared in advance for us to do. 11 Therefore, remember that formerly you who are Gentiles by birth and called "<u>uncircumcised</u>" by those who call themselves "the circumcision" (that done in the body by the hands of men)- 12 remember that at that time <u>you were separate from Christ, excluded from citizenship in Israel and foreigners to the covenants of the promise, without hope and without God in the world.</u> 13 But now in Christ Jesus you who once were far away have been brought near through the blood of Christ.*

If you are a born-again servant of Jesus Christ, you have citizenship in Israel and will remain on earth when the tribulation begins, but you will spend eternity with God in the New Jerusalem.

Nelson's New Illustrated Bible Dictionary defines Israel:

"In the Old Testament, the nation of Israel is referred to as the people of God. ...

In the New Testament, the phrase is used occasionally to describe the "old Israel" (Heb. 1:25). But there is a definite transition to a new covenant and a new people of God, the church, who are now "His own special people" (Titus 2:14) ... .

The church, then, is seen as the new Israel, or true Israel of God (Rom. 9:6; Gal 6:16), the true seed of Abraham (Gal 3:29) and the new people of God (2 Pet. 2:9)" (966).

Do you want to be separated from Israel? No, you don't. The born-again true followers of Christ, the Church, are citizens of Israel and as such will be on earth, not in heaven during the great tribulation.

It should be pointed out that the book of Malachi is addressed to Israel (Jacob).

Malachi 1:1 The burden of the word of the LORD to Israel ....

Malachi 3:10 Bring ye all the tithes into the storehouse ... .

The preceding verses prove that descendants of the ten tribes of Israel, sometimes referred to as Ephraim by the Old Testament prophets, are very much alive and waiting for Bible prophecy to be fulfilled when Christ returns. The Bible prophecy foretold by the prophets cited here can not be fulfilled by Judah alone. This is why you can not look at Israel today and say these prophecies are being fulfilled. When Christ returns He will bring together all 12 tribes, of which the greater part will be Ephraim, just as Hosea prophesied.

Antichrist Comes

14

Just as God visited earth almost 2000 years ago and lived in a body that we call Jesus, the Bible tells us Satan is likewise going to visit earth and live in a body that we call the Antichrist. The Bible also tells us that Jesus is coming again to earth. We have two very important visitations coming: one by God and the other by Satan. The very important question is: **Which one comes first?**

God did not leave us hanging. He answered that question. He told us what to look for before Christ returns. Yes, we do have a sign to let us know how to distinguish between the Antichrist and our Lord and Savior Jesus Christ. Jesus told us that the sign of His coming would be found in the sun, moon and stars.

His coming is referred to as the "day of the Lord". Jesus told us in:

*Matthew 24:29-30 (KJV) **Immediately after the tribulation of those days shall the <u>sun be darkened</u>, and the <u>moon shall not give her light</u>, and the stars shall fall from heaven, and the powers of the heavens shall be shaken: And then shall appear the <u>sign of the Son of man</u> in heaven: and then shall all the tribes of the earth mourn, and they shall see the Son of man coming in the clouds of heaven with power and great glory.***

Remember that *"**Son of man**"* is another name for Jesus. So, if this sign given to us by the sun, moon and stars is not present, then we know that it is not Jesus Christ about to return to earth.

Jesus tells us that when the sun and moon will not give any light is the sign that the "day of the Lord" is *here.* IT IS THE SIGN THAT JESUS CHRIST IS ABOUT TO APPEAR IN THE SKY, IN GREAT POWER AND GLORY.

All the world will see HIM. This is the day the prophets wrote about: It occurs 20 times in 18 verses in the Old Testament.

(Isa 13:6 KJV) Howl ye; for the day of the LORD is at hand; it shall come as a destruction from the Almighty.

(Joel 2:31 KJV) The sun shall be turned into darkness, and the moon into blood, before the great and the terrible day of the LORD come.

(Zep 1:14-15 KJV) *The great day of the LORD is near, it is near, and hasteth greatly, even the voice of the day of the LORD: the mighty man shall cry there bitterly. That day is a day of wrath, a day of trouble and distress, a day of wasteness and desolation, a day of darkness and gloominess, a day of clouds and thick darkness.*

The Apostle Paul spoke about a restraining force that keeps the Antichrist from being revealed (2 Thessalonians 2:4-7). Some have said that it is the Holy Spirit preventing the revealing of the Antichrist, but it is the archangel Michael as seen in Revelation 12:7 (KJV) *And there was war in heaven: Michael and his angels fought against the dragon; and the dragon fought and his angels, 8 And prevailed not; neither was their place found any more in heaven. 9 And the <u>great dragon</u> was cast out, that old serpent, called the Devil, and Satan, which deceiveth the whole world: he was cast out into the earth, and his angels were cast out with him.*

<u>Michael is told by God to cast Satan out of heaven which starts the clock for the 3.5 years of the tribulation.</u>

The prophet Daniel agrees with the Book of Revelation. *Daniel 12:1(NIV) "At that time Michael, the great prince who protects your people, will arise. There will be a time of distress such as has not happened from the beginning of nations until then. But at that time your people—everyone whose name is found written in the book—will be delivered. 2 Multitudes who sleep in the dust of the earth will awake: some to everlasting life, others to shame and everlasting contempt."*

The beast (Antichrist) starts his reign empowered by Satan, the dragon in Rev. 12:9 above. The text continues.

Revelation 13:1 (KJV) *And I stood upon the sand of the sea, and saw <u>a beast</u> rise up out of the sea, having seven heads and ten* *horns, and upon his horns ten crowns, and upon his heads the name of blasphemy.*

And the beast which I saw was like unto a leopard, and his feet were as the feet of a bear, and his mouth as the mouth of a lion: and the <u>dragon gave him his power, and his seat, and great authority</u>.

The revealing of the Antichrist will take place when **God tells Michael, the archangel, to cast Satan out of heaven.** Satan will then empower the Antichrist, the impostor, to begin his 3.5 year reign on earth.

When this impostor makes his debut on the world's stage, it " *... will be in accordance with the work of Satan displayed in all kinds of counterfeit miracles, signs and wonders"* (2 Thessalonians 2:9 NIV). Can you imagine watching the Antichrist on CNN going into the Veterans Hospital in San Antonio and instantly restoring all the missing limbs of so many wounded soldiers and restoring the flesh of the disfigured who had suffered burns in Iraq? Yes, the world will see real miracles performed, not the fake get-out-of-the-wheelchair type, that have turned so many off to the message of the gospel of Jesus Christ.

Remember, Jesus told us ahead of time "the sun will be darkened" before He makes His appearance. With this in mind, Jesus has told us how we can know it is the impostor coming to earth.

Revelation 14:9-11 warns us that those who worship the Antichrist, the man of lawlessness, or receive the "mark of the beast" will be tormented with fire and brimstone eternally. Satan is described as the dragon, the old serpent, and the Devil in Revelation 12:9. The dragon gives power to the beast in Revelation 13:1-2. This same beast is also referred to as the man of sin or the Antichrist. So the "mark of the beast, '666'", is the mark of Satan. Accepting this mark means you will spend eternity with Satan in the "lake of fire". You have been warned.

When you hear of people worshiping this miracle worker, check to see if the sign has been given in the sun, moon and stars. If not then you know the Antichrist, the impostor of Jesus, has arrived.

15 | Jesus Christ Comes

The following depicts the fate of everyone ever born on earth since the beginning of time. It is an enactment of what will happen when Jesus Christ returns to earth. It will be the best of times for those who trusted Christ and have remained faithful to Him. It will be the worst of times for sinners and unbelievers. The names of those judged by Christ are fictional and do not represent anyone living or dead. A young couple, Jim and Sue Savage, both believers of Jesus, give their eyewitness account of the return of Christ in all power and glory. They have endured the horrible days of the tribulation. They have remained true to their God and have not worshiped the beast or taken his mark. Jim and Sue have just finished eating, if you could call it that. They had shared a small bowl of rice and beans. But they are among the more fortunate, because at least they had something to eat. It is one o'clock in the afternoon. Jim was about to get up from the table when he looked outside and noticed it was getting darker. In a few more minutes, he noticed that the sun had turned blood red. A little later, he noticed that it was pitch black outside but that it was still the middle of the day.

Suddenly, Jim shouts, "Sue this is it! This is what we have been waiting for. It's our moment now. The real Jesus is coming soon! This is the Day of the Lord! This is what the Old Testament prophets wrote about! We are going to see it".

Sue had found a flashlight and used it to get to a window. Looking outside, she said, "Jim it's so dark outside. I'm scared. What are we going to do?"

Jim replied, "Don't worry. Soon we should hear a loud trumpet followed by the voice of the archangel and then we shall see the real Jesus Christ, our Lord and Savior, coming down out of the clouds with a multitude of angels!"

Jim shouted "Yes he is coming to save us! Soon, we won't have to suffer. We won't thirst or hunger any more."

Sue prayed, "Thank you Jesus. Thank you Lord."

Soon Jim joined her and they were both on their hands and knees giving thanks to God that their suffering would soon end.

Jim said, "Thank you God that you have given us the strength and courage to endure, for we know that your Word says that 'whoever endures to the end will be saved'".

After a few more moments in prayer, Jim was interrupted by a sound that could be nothing but the trumpet of God. It was so loud that it must have lasted a full minute.

Jim said so excitedly, "Sue, this is it! This is it! This is it! Get ready for the voice of the archangel. It's coming! It's coming! It's next!"

After what seemed like an eternity, they heard a voice that was heard around the world. It very distinctly said, "PREPARE TO MEET YOUR GOD. HE IS COMING."

At this, Jim and Sue were tightly holding on to each other as they looked out the window and up into the sky. It was still pitch black outside. But they stood at the window waiting.

Jim said to Sue, "It won't be long now."

In a few minutes, the sky lit up to a brightness that surpassed the sun shining on the desert on the hottest of days.

They saw a sight that no human had ever seen before. The majesty and glory they looked upon was beyond words. All they could do was look and cry and shout for joy. They were witnessing the return of Jesus Christ in power and glory just like He promised. There were thousands and thousands of angels all in white accompanying Jesus as he slowly descended from the sky. They both were speechless.

The next thing Jim and Sue knew, they were standing in a valley with millions upon millions of people. They were all looking up at a great white throne in front of them. It seemed like one by one the people were being called to come before the One who sat upon the great throne. He was dressed in white and his face radiated purity and light. Millions upon millions looked into the face of their God. It was beyond words to describe how it felt to finally see their God, face to face.

To many, Jesus said, "Enter into my kingdom prepared for you, my good and faithful servant". But it seemed to far more, He was saying, "You are a child of Satan, enter into the fire prepared for him and his angels".

After the judgments of millions more, Sue and Jim heard the name of Leo Landers being called.

The voice of the One on the throne said, "Why did you not listen to your friend Jim? He tried to tell you the truth. Why did you worship the impostor, Jean Le Peut as though he were God? Why did you take his mark? It is written, 'those who take his mark will be punished forever in the lake of fire.' (Revelation 14:9-11). You did just as the Jews when they did not recognize me at my first coming (Luke 19:41). Jim told you many times not to expect me before the sun, moon and stars no longer shine. (Matthew 24:29-30). You listened to man and not the voice of God. You had no love for the truth. Jeremiah warned you about false priests and teachers (Jeremiah 14). Did you not listen to him?"

Then to Leo he said, "Depart from me, you who are cursed, into the eternal fire prepared for the devil and his angels" (Matthew 25:41).

After the individual judgments of millions more, Sue and Jim heard the name of the famous TV evangelist, Sam Wynner, being called and the voice of the One on the throne say to the archangel Gabriel, "Tell him how many souls will spend eternity with him in hell because he did not warn them to expect the impostor before My return. They were sheep without a shepherd. All he did was tell them that God wanted them to be rich. Where is that in my Word?"

Jesus looked at one of His many angels and said, "Bring Paul to me".

Instantly, Paul appeared and Jesus said, "Tell him what you wrote about the love of money".

Paul started speaking:

... These are the things you are to teach and insist on. If anyone teaches otherwise and does not agree to the sound instruction of our Lord Jesus Christ and to godly teaching, they are conceited and understand nothing. ... For we brought nothing into the world, and we can take nothing out of it. But if we have food and clothing, we will be content with that. Those who want to get rich fall into temptation and a trap and into many foolish and harmful desires that plunge people into ruin and destruction. For the love of money is a root of all kinds of evil. Some people, eager for money, have wandered from the faith and pierced themselves with many griefs. (1 Timothy 6:2-10 TNIV).

Jesus said, "Thank you, Paul".

Then He looked into the eyes of Sam and said, "You did not teach these things. You did not warn your flock to not expect Me until after the sign was given in the sun, moon and stars".

Jesus called out, "Bring up Peter".

Peter appeared.

Jesus said, "Peter tell everyone what you spoke on the day of Pentecost about when I would come again".

Peter began to speak, "I told them, 'The sun will be turned to darkness and the moon to blood before the coming of the great and glorious day of the Lord'" (Acts 2:20 NIV).

Jesus said, "Thank you, Peter".

Jesus then told Sam, "Why did you not warn your people to look to the sun and moon as the sign of My return? This is the 'day of the Lord' that Peter just spoke about. It is also what Joel, Isaiah, Amos, Obadiah, Zephaniah, Zechariah and Paul wrote about".

Jesus continued, "When I was speaking with My Disciples, I answered the question: 'what will be the sign of your coming?' when I said:

"Immediately after the tribulation of those days shall the sun be darkened, and the moon shall not give her light, and the stars shall fall from heaven, and the powers of the heavens shall be shaken: And then shall appear the sign of the Son of man in heaven" (Matthew 24:29-30).

Jesus then asked Sam, "Why did you ignore the warnings of those seven prophets and also my warning?" Jesus then said, "Depart from Me".

Sue looked at Jim and said, "Wow, can you believe what we just witnessed?"

Jim replied, "The Bible says the preachers will be judged more harshly than others will".

After the judgments of millions more, Sue and Jim heard the name of Bill Bennzer, who was the pastor of the church they attended, that is, before the tribulation began, being called.

Then they heard the voice of the One on the throne say, "I am well pleased with you Bill. You did not stray from the truth in my Word. You warned your flock not to expect Me until after the sign was given in the sun, moon and stars. You will receive your reward. Enter into my kingdom".

Sue said to Jim, "I knew he would be rewarded".

After a while, Sue and Jim heard the name of Jerome Snoders being called.

Sue looked at Jim and said, "I remember him. He's that preacher in Houston that had the building program that went on forever. He was always building and always asking for more money".

Jim said "Yes, I don't think he ever understood that people should come to hear the Word of God and they don't all have to be together in some large expensive building. He had seven assistant pastors. Why couldn't they break up into smaller groups and listen to one of the assistants read the Word?"

Sue chimed in, "Yes, but it's all about seeing 'the man' on Sunday morning".

Jim spoke up, "You know, the building program I remember, was when Paul said the Church was: "built on the foundation of the apostles and prophets, with Christ Jesus himself as the chief cornerstone. In him the whole building is joined together and rises to become a holy temple in the Lord" (Ephesians 2:20-21 NIV).

Sue replied, "Jim, I think Jesus was more interested in people rather than buildings, because He said many times to help the poor".

Jesus looked at Jerome and said, "Why did you neglect your

doctrine? All you could think about was more buildings".

Jesus said, "Bring up Paul".

In an instant Paul appeared again.

Jesus said, "Paul tell him what you said about watching your doctrine".

Paul, looking directly into the eyes of Jerome, said, "Watch your life and doctrine closely. Persevere in them, because if you do, you will save both yourself and your hearers" (1 Timothy 4:16 NIV).

Jesus said, "Jerome, you did not do this. You did not preach the whole truth, like you used to. You will receive no rewards for your buildings".

The archangel Michael looked at the angel Gabriel and asked, "Do you think hell is going to be large enough, or do we need to start a building program?"

Works Cited

Church, Leslie F., ed. Commentary on the Whole Bible by Matthew Henry. Grand Rapids: Zondervan, 1961

Clarke, Adam. Clarke's Commentary. 6 vols. New York: Abingdon-Cokesbury Press.

Clarke, Adam. Clarke's Commentary. March 2, 2009.

<http://www.godrules.net/library/clarke/clarke2the2.htm>,

Clogg, F. Bertram, The Abington Bible Commentary. Ed. Eiselen, F.C., Lewis, E., Downey, D.G. New York: Abingdon Press, 1929.

Dockery, David, ed. Holman Bible Handbook. Nashville: Holman Bible Publishers, 1992.

Farrar, F.W. Life and Work of St. Paul. London: Cassell and Company, 1879.

Graham, Billy. Storm Warning. Dallas: Word Publishing, 1992.

Halley, Henry H. Halley's Bible Handbook. Grand Rapids: Zondervan Publishing, 1965

Henry, Matthew, Matthew Henry's Concise Commentary. Grand Rapids: Zondervan, 1961

Henry, Matthew, Matthew Henry's Concise Commentary. Christiansunite. 3 March, 2009 <http://bible.christiansunite.com/mhcc.cgi?b=Da&c=9>

Historical Estimates of World Population. Oct. 16, 2008. U.S. Census Bureau. <www.census.gov/ipc/www/worldhis.html> May 2, 2009.

Jamieson, Fausett & Brown Commentary on The Whole Bible. Grand Rapids: Zondervan Publishing House, 1961

LaHaye, Tim. Revelation Unveiled. Grand Rapids: Zondervan Publishing House, 1999.

Life Application Bible. Wheaton: Tyndale House Publishers, 1991.

New American Bible, New York: Catholic Book Publishing Co., 1992

Open Bible, Nashville:Nelson, 1998.

Pink, Arthur W. Exposition of The Gospel John. Grand Rapids: Zondervan, 1945.

Riley, W.B. The Bible of the Expositor And The Evangelist, Daniel. Cleveland: Union Gospel Press, 1933.

Rist, Martin. The Interpreter's Bible. 12 vols. Nashville: Abington Press, 1957.

Rosenthal, Marvin. The Pre-Wrath Rapture Of The Church. Nashville: Thomas Nelson, 1990.

Scofield, C. I., The Scofield Reference Bible. London:Oxford, 1917.

Summers, Ray. Worthy Is The Lamb. Nashville: Broadman Press,1951

Wuest, Kenneth S., The New Testament An Expanded Translation. Grand Rapids: Eerdmans, 1961

Young, Robert. Young's Literal Translation. London: Pickering & Inglis, 1862.

Youngblood, Ronald F., ed. Nelson's New Illustrated Bible Dictionary. Nashville: Nelson, 1995.